Write EVERY DAY

178
Reproducible Research and
Writing Activities

Write EVERY DAY

178 Reproducible Research and Writing Activities

by Jane Schall
illustrated by Patricia Briles

SCHOLASTIC
PROFESSIONAL BOOKS

New York • Toronto • London • Aukland • Sydney

Write Every Day was edited by Rosemary Alexander.

JS: To Judy Cohn, who truly loves books and is a wonderful person to work with

PB: To my Mom and Dad, who always believed in me

Table of Contents

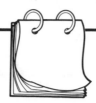

Edgar Rice Burroughs

Happy Birthday, Mr. Burroughs! Who was Mr. Burroughs? He was the creator of Tarzan, one of the most famous book characters in the world. Everyone knows Tarzan and that he was "the king of the jungle." Here's your chance to describe the jungle. Pretend that you are in charge of inviting people to visit the jungle. First of all, choose the particular jungle you want them to visit. Somewhere in Africa? The Amazon in South America? Conduct a little research, then put your research and writing skills to the test. Develop a travel folder that will make everyone want to spend his or her next vacation in a deep, dark !and. This type of writing is called persuasive writing. Use as many interesting and exciting adjectives and phrases as possible. Here's a blank brochure. Use it, or make your own.

Ramadan

The ninth month of the Islamic calendar is called Ramadan. When the new moon appears at the beginning of this month, people in many Muslim countries begin a month of fasting. They do not let anything touch their lips from sunrise to sunset —no food, water, or cigarettes. They spend much of their time praying.

Ramadan has been observed for 1,300 years. The Muslim holy book, the Koran, states that fasting and prayer quiet the spirit and discipline the soul. People of many religions pray to quiet their souls. And almost everyone agrees that when you are calm inside it's easier to think and to concentrate.

What are some ways you can calm yourself inside? Does it help to sit outside and listen to the wind? Or to curl up alone in a quiet corner and listen to your own breathing?

Use the chart below to list ways that you think might help you to feel calm inside. Then ask other people—adults and your friends—to suggest ways that work for them.

During the next week or two, try at least five different ways to feel calm inside and tell how you felt. Keep this chart as a record to help remind you and to write down other ways that work for you.

A Calming Chart

Ways that work for me: _____

_____

_____

_____

_____

Date and results: _____

_____

_____

_____

_____

Ways that work for others: _____

_____

_____

_____

_____

What happened when I tried: _____

_____

_____

_____

_____

To me, being calm means _____

_____

_____

September 3, 1939

World War II Declaration Anniversary

On this day in 1939, British prime minister Neville Chamberlain announced in a radio broadcast that England was declaring war against Germany.

Pretend you're a newspaper or radio reporter; it's your job to explain this event to the public. But you have to understand it before you can describe it. Use encyclopedias or other resource books to help you answer the following questions:

1. What country was Germany invading at the time? _____

2. Which other countries also issued declarations of war? _____

3. Who was Winston Churchill? _____

4. Why was he important to this time period? _____

_____

5. Who was the president of the United States at this time? _____

_____

6. When did the United States enter the war? _____

7. What were the troops who were fighting against Germany called? What were the opposing troops called?

_____

8. Who was the leader of Germany? _____

9. How long did the war last? _____

10. List three other facts you didn't know about the war that you discovered during your research.

_____

_____

_____

September 5, 1897

Arthur Charles Nielsen's Birthday

And who was Arthur Charles Nielsen? In 1923 he founded a company that has become well known for its radio and television audience surveys. Nielsen's company tries to decide what shows are the most popular so that stations and networks can choose which ones to continue and which ones to cancel. This is also useful information for advertisers.

Conduct a survey of your own. Choose a particular time and day of the week, such as Thursday, 8:00 to 8:30 p.m. Record the time on the "Audience Survey" sheets, and list the programs that are on at that time in your particular area. Now poll many different people: entire families, boys and girls your age, parents, young children. Ask at least five people in each age category what show they watch during that particular time period. Record their answers on the survey chart provided, or make your own chart.

Then summarize the results so that your survey can be easily understood. (You might want to compare your results with others in your class, or arrange for pairs of pollsters to cover specific time periods so that the whole week is covered. Then your results will include a week's worth of TV viewing in your community.)

Audience Survey

TV ratings in my town: _____
(fill in the name)

Time period: _____

Day of the week: _____

Target audience: _____

Name: _____ Preference: _____

Summary of survey results: _____

_____

How might advertisers use this information? _____

_____

_____

September 6, 1899

Billy Rose's Birthday

Billy Rose was a famous songwriter, author, and theatrical producer. Some of his best-loved songs include "That Old Gang of Mine," "Me and My Shadow," and "Without a Song." These songs and others have continued to bring many people great pleasure, even after his death in 1966.

A song is like a gift. It tells someone something important, brings great joy, or simply provides terrific music to listen or dance to. The lyrics of the song are the words.

Think of your five favorite songs. List them here.

1. _____
2. _____
3. _____
4. _____
5. _____

Do they have anything in common? How are they alike? How are they different? _____

What kind of music do you most like to listen to? What kind of lyrics do you like? In honor of Billy Rose and all the other composers who have given the gift of music to the world, try your hand at songwriting. Use a melody that is familiar to you, or make one up yourself. What kind of song would you like to write? Will it have a refrain? Will the verses tell a story? Use the back of this page as a worksheet. Writing a song is much like writing a poem; you need to use rhythm and melody to make the words flow. Keep it simple at first; add more details later. (To get into the mood, you might want to listen to a few of your favorite tunes.)

September 7, 1936

Buddy Holly's Birthday

Buddy Holly (born Charles Hardin Holley) was an important American musical composer. He will be remembered as a pioneer of rock music. Two of his big hits were "Peggy Sue" and "That'll Be the Day." But his career ended tragically when he died in an airplane crash at the age of 22. No one will ever know what other accomplishments he might have had if he had lived longer.

Can you think of other people who died before they could accomplish all that they had set out to do? Two might be John F. Kennedy and Martin Luther King, Jr.

Choose one of the three people mentioned on this page. Then pick someone else you know of and admire. Read more about both of your choices. Then use what you've discovered to help you answer the following:

Names: _____

_____

What was each person famous for? _____

_____

What special qualities helped him or her to accomplish something in particular? _____

_____

How did these people influence others? _____

_____

What did they have in common? _____

_____

Choose one person and think about that person's life. What might that person have accomplished if he or she had lived longer?

_____

_____

_____

September 10

Swap Ideas Day

To celebrate this day, use the space below to write down at least ten good ideas. These can be anything that makes a lot of sense to you—something you've heard from someone else or something you've thought of yourself. You might want to include safety tips (Don't clean up broken glass with your bare hands); good health tips (Don't eat a candy bar right before you go to bed, after you've brushed your teeth); or get-happy tips (Try to smile, even if you're sad; things won't seem so bad!).

1. _____
2. _____
3. _____
4. _____
5. _____
6. _____
7. _____
8. _____
9. _____
10. _____

After you've completed your list, share your common sense with others by adding them to a class list of ideas.

The Sunday Following Labor Day (September)

National Grandparents Day

Pretend that you are a grandparent. You have had children and now your children have children. Use the space below and on the back of this page to write a story about your life for them to read. Describe yourself: the things you like to do, your accomplishments, and the things you would still like to accomplish. Talk about your family, your hopes and dreams, your fondest memories, and your friendships.

As you write, think about what you hope the world will be like, and how you hope it will treat people of your generation. End your story with some words of wisdom from one who has lived a long time.

September 12, 1913

Jesse Owens's Birthday

James Cleveland Owens was a great American athlete. He set 11 world records in track and field. At one meet he broke five world records and tied another, all in the span of 45 minutes! He won four gold medals at the 1936 Olympic games.

Look up and read about Jesse Owens and the 1936 Berlin Olympics in a reference book. Use the space below to report the story of his achievements for a U.S. newspaper. Include facts about how Jesse Owens became a hero to the German people.

Headline: _____

Who: _____

Where: _____

When: _____

What happened: _____

_____

_____

_____

_____

Why: _____

_____

_____

_____

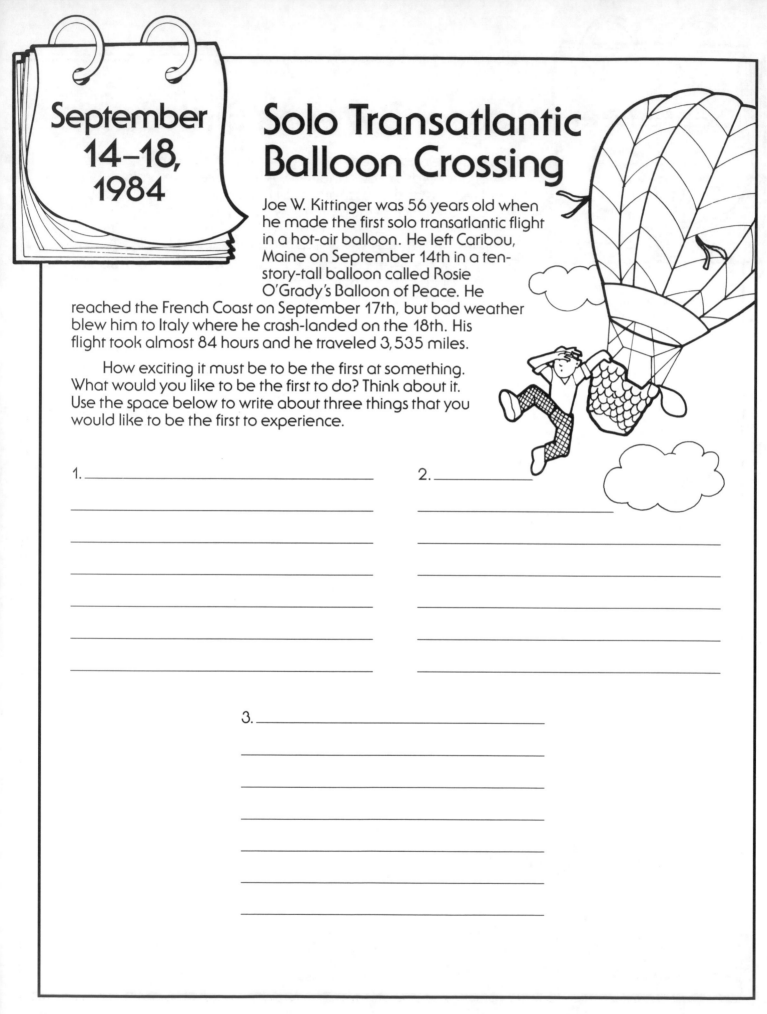

September 14–18, 1984

Solo Transatlantic Balloon Crossing

Joe W. Kittinger was 56 years old when he made the first solo transatlantic flight in a hot-air balloon. He left Caribou, Maine on September 14th in a ten-story-tall balloon called Rosie O'Grady's Balloon of Peace. He reached the French Coast on September 17th, but bad weather blew him to Italy where he crash-landed on the 18th. His flight took almost 84 hours and he traveled 3,535 miles.

How exciting it must be to be the first at something. What would you like to be the first to do? Think about it. Use the space below to write about three things that you would like to be the first to experience.

1. _____

2. _____

3. _____

September 15, 1890

Agatha Christie's Birthday

Agatha Christie, born in Torquay, England, wrote more than 100 mysteries. Some of her stories have been adapted for television, the theater, and movies. What is a mystery? Every mystery has a crime, some important clues, a person who commits the crime, and a person who solves the mystery.

Try your hand at mystery writing. Use the space below and on the back of this page to develop a mysterious character. Decide whether it will be male or female; the person's age; physical characteristics; peculiar personality traits; odd background. Does he or she have a simple name or an unusual one? Will this character arouse the suspicion of others or be able to slip in and out of places unnoticed? Is this character someone who solves the crimes of others—or commits them?

Pretend that you are on a long train ride and you spot this character across the dining car. You run to get your friend but when you return, the character is gone! How would you describe the person to your friend? Before you write, remember: you want your friend to be able to absolutely identify this character.

Write A Mystery!

Now try writing a mystery! As you may know, the author of a mystery usually provides clues along the way. Follow this plan:

1. Decide on at least five main characters and choose names for all of them. Include the character you just created.

2. Pick a setting for your story (describe it as carefully as you can, perhaps a huge, overgrown garden where the bushes form a maze in which a person could get lost).

3. Choose personalities for your characters, tell what they do, and how they are connected to one another.

4. Decide who will be the victim.

5. Use the following clues in any order to help construct your story: a rusty old bicycle with a flat tire; a cut telephone cord; a ring of old keys; a secret passageway. (And, of course, add your own clues.)

6. Try to make the ending a surprise to the reader, but also one that ties up all the loose ends.

7. Share your story with your class. Compare stories to see how others used the same clues to create totally different stories.

September 17–23

Constitution Week

As a citizen of the United States, you are protected by the Constitution. A constitution is a document that contains a system of principles by which a country is governed. The laws laid out by the U.S. Constitution give citizens the power to govern their country.

Pretend that you are one of the first members of a space colony and you need to create a constitution. Use the space below and on the back of this paper to write a paragraph about the kinds of laws your colony needs. Then list five to ten laws that the colonists must obey in order to live together peacefully.

Once your laws are written, compare them with other students' and share the best ones. You might want to work on a class constitution for Space Colony No. 1, U.S.A.

Laws: _____

_____

_____

_____

_____

_____

_____

_____

_____

_____

_____

_____

_____

_____

_____

Third Tuesday in September

International Day of Peace

The United Nations General Assembly has created this day to strengthen the ideas of peace among all nations and people. Some people have suggested that a University for Peace would be one way to strengthen these ideas.

Suppose you are a student at this university and are studying five courses. These courses are listed below:

1. International Law
2. Problem Solving
3. Modern World History
4. Ways to Communicate
5. The Work of the UN

On the lines below, write one reason why you think each course is important in working for peace. On the last line suggest another course that would be important to study.

1. _____
   _____

2. _____
   _____

3. _____
   _____

4. _____
   _____

5. _____
   _____

6. _____
   _____

September 22 or 23

It's Autumn!

Autumn begins in the Northern Hemisphere! And for many people this is the official beginning of their favorite season. What do you think of when you think of fall? The smell of leaves, or maybe a crunching sound? The crisp morning air? The patterns and designs of the first frost? The glow of jack-o'-lanterns smiling? Make a list of other autumn words and phrases. List colors, sights, smells, and sounds below.

Now use these word pictures and phrases to write a poem containing at least two pairs of rhyming lines. If you live in a part of the country where autumn leaves do not change color, write a poem that describes fall where you live or one about how you imagine autumn to be. Write on the back of this page or another sheet of paper.

_____

_____

_____

_____

_____

_____

_____

_____

_____

_____

_____

_____

_____

_____

First Ice-Cream Cone

Italo Marchiony came to New York City from Italy in the late 1800s. He had a pushcart and used it to sell lemon ice. Soon he had a whole fleet of pushcarts and decided to develop a special paper cone to hold the ice. The paper didn't work well, so he developed a pastry cone. On this day he applied for a patent for his ice-cream-cone mold! A U.S. patent was issued to him a few months later.

Celebrate this day by eating an ice-cream cone in his honor. Also remember him by creating a fanciful tale about a magical ice-cream cone. Here's one way to begin:

It was a very warm August afternoon—a very, very warm August afternoon. No air conditioning anywhere in town was working, so all the stores were closed and the people had gone home. Ice in the ice machines was melting, soda was warm, and Jerome could feel a long trickle of sweat roll down his back from his neck to his waist. He needed something cool.

With a dollar in his pocket and not much hope in his heart, Jerome headed toward the ice-cream store. Sure enough, all the lights were off; Mr. Simpson had gone home and probably all those buckets of ice cream were just swimming there like soup. Peering closer through the window, Jerome thought he saw a glow. What would be glowing in Mr. Simpson's ice-cream store? And why did the door look like it was open just a crack? He dared himself to pull it open slowly; the rush of cool air sent a sudden shiver down his spine. Jerome started to walk inside... (Okay, now it's your turn!)

_____

_____

_____

_____

_____

_____

_____

_____

September 26, 1774

Johnny Appleseed's Birthday

Let's celebrate! John Chapman, otherwise known as Johnny Appleseed, is thought to have been born on this date. He was a roving pioneer who distributed herbs and medicinal plants. But he is best known for planting apple orchards that are still thriving today in Ohio and Indiana.

Compile an apple cookbook in his honor. Think about your favorite apple recipe— apple cobbler, apple crisp, apple cake, apple sauce, or good ol' apple pie. Check cookbooks for unusual recipes made with apples or ask a relative for a favorite family recipe. Now use the recipe card below to write (and illustrate) your favorite recipe. Compile these as a class, make copies, and distribute them in honor of this special American.

Recipe name: _____

Contributor: _____

Source: _____

Ingredients: _____

_____

Instructions: _____

_____

_____

_____

October

Stamp Collecting Month

What is the word for a stamp collector? *Philatelist.* This term comes from two Greek words: *philos*, meaning loving, and *atelos*, which means free of tax. (Stamps are a sign that postage has been paid on a piece of mail, and no more tax is due on it.) Therefore, putting these meanings together, a philatelist studies stamps, is someone who loves to study stamps—their history, their paper and ink, their artwork and design, and the printing process.

Many stamps honor or commemorate an event or famous person. On its first day of issue, the U.S. Postal Service sells a stamp in only one selected city. A First Day Cover is an envelope bearing a stamp canceled in the selected city.

Design your own stamp. First choose an event or a famous person you would like to commemorate. Use the space below to record a few important facts about your subject:

Subject: _____

_____

_____

Research: _____

_____

_____

_____

_____

_____

_____

Now it's time to design the stamp itself. Many stamps come in blocks of four or a series. If your subject is adaptable, you might even want to design more than one stamp on the same theme. Remember, details are very important to philatelists. Think about the borders, colors, even an appropriate phrase. Stamp designers draw their stamps quite large; printers then reduce the final art to stamp size.

The First Week in October

Fire Prevention Week

Celebrate this week by doing your part to help prevent injuries from fires. Use the space below to write a 30-second spot (commercial) to present over your school's public address system. Before you begin, think about what you already know about fire safety. Next, ask your librarian for information on fire prevention and safety.

     Now write the script. You might want to develop parts for more people than just you. Also, don't forget possible sound effects. Skits can be humorous, but you do have important points to get across. Practice your spot so it goes smoothly. Time yourself—be careful not to go too fast, or your audience won't understand your words.

October 2, 1869

Mohandas "Mahatma" Gandhi's Birthday

Mahatma means "great soul," and many people call this famous man by that name. Gandhi lived in India. He helped free his country from English rule through his strong belief in nonviolent methods, gathering large groups of people to march or sit in peaceful protest. He would fast (not eat) for days to draw attention to a particular problem and would rather go to jail than obey a law he thought was unfair. He truly believed that he could change the world for the better without physically harming anyone.

Can you think of other people in history who have believed in nonviolent protest? Can you think of times in history when this type of action might have worked? In your community? In your personal life? Use the space below and the back of this page to record these times.

Then ask other people if they can remember instances when nonviolence worked. Ask older people if they ever participated in any kind of nonviolent protests and what the outcomes were. Share your findings with your class. Discuss how this action might help to solve important problems today.

Thor Heyerdahl's Birthday

Thor Heyerdahl was born in Larvik, Norway. He became very interested in the islands of the Pacific Ocean and visited a small island called Fatu Hiva. While he was there he studied the people and the ancient ruins of the island. Heyerdahl had the idea that these people had sailed to the island from South America. Many people thought he was wrong—that people in earlier times wouldn't have had boats strong enough to make the trip. Heyerdahl decided to prove he was right. He had a raftlike boat built out of balsa wood. Named the *Kon-Tiki,* his boat was 45 feet long and much like those of the ancient South Americans. With his crew of five men, he set out from South America in April, 1947. One hundred and one days later he reached the island! He proved that the ancient people could have migrated in such a way.

For as long as people have existed, men and women have looked for adventure. Is there an adventure that you long for? You don't have to be the first person ever to have done it, nor must you risk your life. But the adventure must be a challenge—something that gives you a sense of excitement.

What would seem like a wonderful adventure to you? Describe it here and on the back of this page.

_____

_____

_____

_____

_____

_____

_____

_____

_____

National Storytelling Festival

Master storytellers from all over the United States gather together in Jonesborough, Tennessee, this week to tell and exchange stories. In honor of this event, hold a storytelling festival right in your classroom! Learn a favorite story; know it so well that you can tell it without reading it or looking at any of the worlds. Then tell it to a group, include events or incidents that might have happened, change the inflection of your voice dramatically, and add sound effects. All of these ideas will keep your audience attentive and excited.

Writing cooperative stories is another interesting activity for this week. Ask two or three friends to work with you. Each of you writes the beginning of a story, stopping just before something is about to happen. Then pass the papers to the friend on the right who continues your story until something else is about to happen. Pass the papers to the right again. Continue until you get your story beginning back; then finish the tale. When the stories are completed, take turns reading them to each other so everyone can see how his or her sentences became part of your story.

This paragraph may help you get started, or try to think of your own idea.

Nikki couldn't think of a thing to do. Homework? No way. Call up a friend? Not now; it was too close to dinnertime. Ride her bike? Nope; she had that flat tire and didn't feel like fixing it. So she slumped on the couch, feeling very bored. Just then the doorbell rang...

The First Monday in October

Universal Children's Day

The United Nations General Assembly has established this important day to foster understanding among children all over the world. The United Nations International Children's Fund (UNICEF) promotes this day in more than 120 countries around the world. In fact, UNICEF helps provide nutrition, education, and emergency care to almost one million children! One of the ways you can help UNICEF help others is to join the "Trick or Treat for UNICEF" program. At Halloween time, children dress in costumes and go "trick or treating" for money to help UNICEF carry out its work.

Ask your librarian for information about the program and then write three reasons why you think everyone should join the program. Use your best persuasive writing.

1. _____

2. _____

3. _____

If your school or youth group is part of the program, make a poster to advertise it. Include your reasons on the poster.

_____

_____

_____

_____

_____

_____

_____

_____

_____

_____

Martina Navratilova's Birthday

Martina Navratilova is one of the most skillful tennis players in the world. She was born in Prague, Czechoslovakia, and was already a tennis star when she came to live in the United States. Martina has earned millions of dollars from tournaments and has set up the Martina Foundation to share some of her wealth with poor children. The foundation gives scholarships so needy children can get an education; it also provides money for tennis lessons and trips to tennis matches.

Many other athletes have set up similar foundations to help others. Dave Winfield, the baseball outfielder, has a foundation to help fight drugs. When his team travels to games in other cities, he always makes sure that he visits schools in those areas and speaks against drugs.

If you were a professional athlete, in which sport would you like to excel? Pretend that you are tops in that sport. With the money you've earned, you decide that you are going to set up a foundation. Name your foundation and explain what you would do with the money. In what other ways would you help people?

Use this space to describe your foundation and your role in it. What kinds of things would you do besides give money?

Foundation: _____

_____

_____

_____

Description: _____

_____

_____

_____

_____

My part: _____

_____

_____

ISBN 0-590-49075-3
Copyright © 1990 by Scholastic Inc. All rights reserved.
12 11 10 9 8 7 6   4 5/9
                                                      34
Printed in the U.S.A.
Write Every Day was edited by Rosemary Alexander.

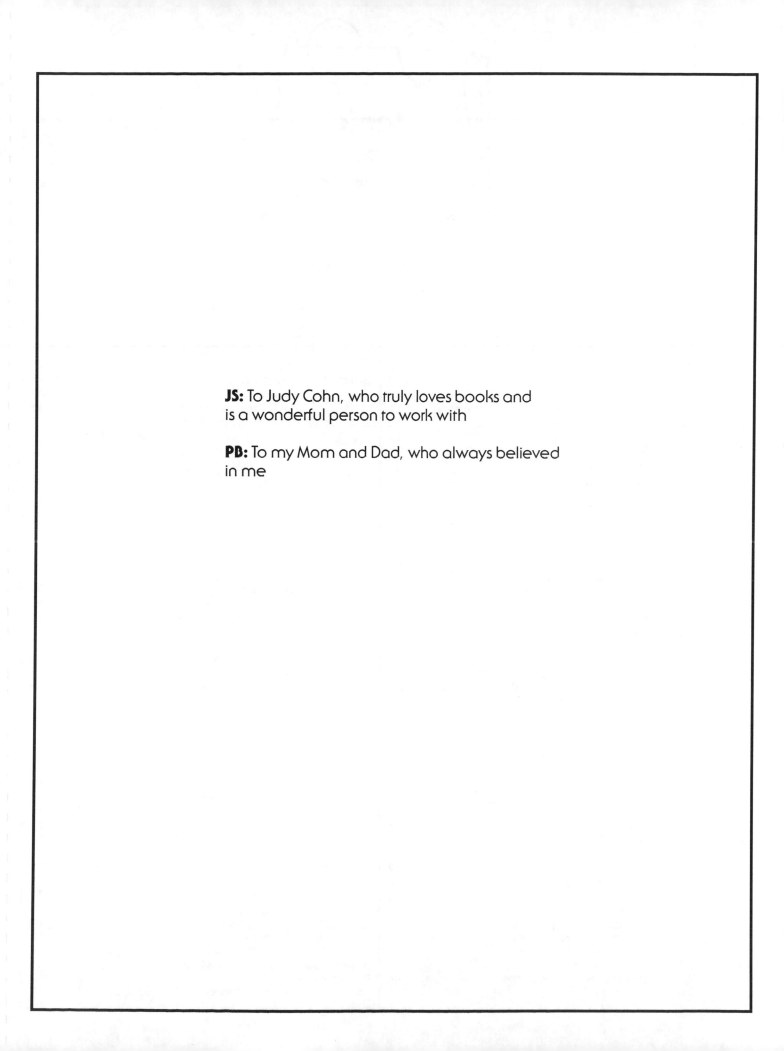

September 1, 1875

Edgar Rice Burroughs

Happy Birthday, Mr. Burroughs! Who was Mr. Burroughs? He was the creator of Tarzan, one of the most famous book characters in the world. Everyone knows Tarzan and that he was "the king of the jungle." Here's your chance to describe the jungle. Pretend that you are in charge of inviting people to visit the jungle. First of all, choose the particular jungle you want them to visit. Somewhere in Africa? The Amazon in South America? Conduct a little research, then put your research and writing skills to the test. Develop a travel folder that will make everyone want to spend his or her next vacation in a deep, dark land. This type of writing is called persuasive writing. Use as many interesting and exciting adjectives and phrases as possible. Here's a blank brochure. Use it, or make your own.

September 22, 1903

First Ice-Cream Cone

Italo Marchiony came to New York City from Italy in the late 1800s. He had a pushcart and used it to sell lemon ice. Soon he had a whole fleet of pushcarts and decided to develop a special paper cone to hold the ice. The paper didn't work well, so he developed a pastry cone. On this day he applied for a patent for his ice-cream-cone mold! A U.S. patent was issued to him a few months later.

Celebrate this day by eating an ice-cream cone in his honor. Also remember him by creating a fanciful tale about a magical ice-cream cone. Here's one way to begin:

It was a very warm August afternoon—a very, very warm August afternoon. No air conditioning anywhere in town was working, so all the stores were closed and the people had gone home. Ice in the ice machines was melting, soda was warm, and Jerome could feel a long trickle of sweat roll down his back from his neck to his waist. He needed something cool.

With a dollar in his pocket and not much hope in his heart, Jerome headed toward the ice-cream store. Sure enough, all the lights were off; Mr. Simpson had gone home and

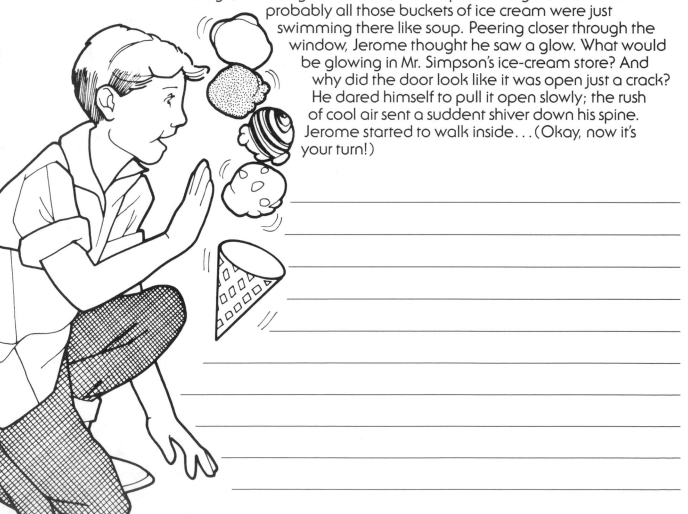

probably all those buckets of ice cream were just swimming there like soup. Peering closer through the window, Jerome thought he saw a glow. What would be glowing in Mr. Simpson's ice-cream store? And why did the door look like it was open just a crack? He dared himself to pull it open slowly; the rush of cool air sent a suddent shiver down his spine. Jerome started to walk inside...(Okay, now it's your turn!)

_____

_____

_____

_____

_____

_____

_____

Thanksgiving

The Pilgrims

News flash: This is_____, at Plymouth Rock where the pilgrims have just docked the *Mayflower*. The people are coming off the boat now. Wait a minute, it looks like we'll have a chance to interview one of the passengers. What an opportunity! Ladies and gentlemen, let me introduce you to...

Whom would you pick to interview? A boy or girl your age? The captain of the ship? What questions would you ask? Use the space below to record both your questions and the person's answers.

Remember that a good interviewer gets as many facts as possible and thinks about what his or her audience would want to know. Make sure you include whom you are interviewing; what kinds of things that person saw and did on the trip; what he or she plans to do in the new land; and how that person felt during the voyage. Try to draw out the person's feelings and thoughts.

Name of person interviewed: _____

Age: _____   Additional information about the person: _____

Question: _____

Answer: _____

_____

Question: _____

Answer: _____

_____

Question: _____

Answer: _____

_____

Your concluding remarks to the audience: _____

_____

_____

_____

November 23, 1887

Boris Karloff's Birthday

Boris Karloff was one of the most famous horror-movie actors of all time. He played the monster in *Frankenstein* and in *The Mummy.* Karloff was so scary that many moviegoers couldn't bear to look and some would leave the theater! Still others complained of nightmares after seeing his performances.

Nightmares can certainly be scary, but it's good to talk about them—even if it's just to yourself. Use the space below as a private space to write about a nightmare you have had—or one that you hope you never do have! You may want to draw or paint your nightmare on some drawing paper.

If you would rather stay away from the subject of nightmares altogether, use the space below to write your own horror-movie plot. Be as descriptive as you can and don't forget to add notes about strange sound effects!

November 25, 1914

Joe DiMaggio's Birthday

This famous New York Yankee baseball player set a major league record that still hasn't been broken—he hit safely in 56 consecutive games! He is considered one of baseball's greatest players and is a member of the Baseball Hall of Fame.

Many sports have a hall of fame, a memorial to the greatest players of that game. Usually there are rules to help determine who is eligible for membership. Look in an encyclopedia to find the rules for membership in the Baseball Hall of Fame.

Start your own hall of fame. First, decide what it will be for—famous explorers, adventurers, animal lovers, maybe even animals, and so on.

Hall of Fame

Next, decide the rules for election, such as a number of years in the profession, extraordinary accomplishment, and so on.

1. _____
2. _____
3. _____
4. _____
5. _____

Also decide who will submit nominations, and who will vote for final membership.

Last of all, nominate at least three candidates for your first induction. Be sure to give reasons for each.

Nominee:_____ Reason:_____

Nominee:_____ Reason:_____

Nominee:_____ Reason:_____

Nominee:_____ Reason:_____

Nominee:_____ Reason:_____

Nominee:_____ Reason:_____

_____
_____

November 26, 1922

Charles Schultz's Birthday

Mr. Schultz's famous cartoon figures, Lucy, Linus, Snoopy, Charlie Brown, and all the gang are 40 years old. And we all love their special personalities and characteristics.

Create your own cartoon character. Think about the cartoon characters you like best. What makes them so appealing? Combine some of those features with any other ideas you have and list the characteristics of your new character here:

_____

_____

Mickey may be a mouse, and Snoopy a dog, but we often forget that because these characters seem human. What animal would you choose to make a second character?

_____

What are your two characters' names? _____

_____

Describe their personalities. _____

_____

Who else might be involved in their adventures?

_____

_____

What are some of the things your characters do to make you laugh? What adventures could your characters go on?

_____

Use the back of this sheet or another piece of paper to draw a comic strip about your characters. If you have a hard time thinking of a joke to include, use a funny riddle you've heard.

December 1, 1955

Rosa Parks Day

One day in 1955, Rosa Parks did a very brave thing. She sat down in a front seat of a Montgomery, Alabama, city bus. In 1955 in Montgomery and other parts of the South, city buses were segregated—the front seats were reserved for whites; African-Americans had to sit in the back. The driver of the bus asked Rosa Parks to move to the back and she refused. Rosa Parks was arrested for her action on December 1, 1955. As a result, African-American people in the city refused to ride the buses until they were no longer segregated. They also began to boycott (refuse to buy from) white businesses. These brave, nonviolent actions helped to bring about the civil rights movement in this country.

What does civil rights mean? The dictionary will tell you that it refers to the rights a person has because he or she is a citizen or a member of society. You are a member of society. What rights do you have? Where do the rights come from? What or who protects your civil rights? Use the space below to write a definition of civil rights in your own words. Tell about some of the rights you have and how they are protected. Do you agree with what Rosa Parks did? Can you think of other people in history who fought (nonviolently) and helped to further the cause of civil rights?

_____

_____

_____

_____

_____

_____

_____

_____

_____

_____

BOYCOTT

December 3, 1755

Gilbert Stuart's Birthday

When you think of pictures of George Washington, does a particular one come to mind? Chances are it is the painting of his face that hangs in schools and public buildings all over the country. This famous portrait was painted by Gilbert Stuart. Born in Rhode Island, he became America's favorite portrait painter by the time he was 35 years old.

A portrait is a picture of a person. It may be drawn, painted, or photographed. There is also something called a self-portrait, which is a person's drawing of himself or herself.

Try it! Take a good look at yourself in the mirror and study your features. Do you have large eyes? What kind of eyebrows do you have? How wide and high is your forehead? How long is your nose? Smile. Are your teeth showing? Do you have a long or short chin? Is your face long and narrow? Round? Heart-shaped? Look at your ears; what other features are they even with?

Use the space below to answer these questions and to add any other descriptions of yourself. After you have completed your description in words, you might want to read it to a friend and ask if he or she has anything to add.

And now it's time. On a separate piece of paper, try doing a self-portrait. You can always refer back to your notes, to a mirror, or to a friend. Have fun!

December 3, 1984

Bhopal Poison Gas Disaster

Put on your investigative reporter hats. On this day a very sad event occurred in Bhopal, India. More than 2,000 persons were killed and more than 200,000 more were injured by a leak of deadly gas. It was the world's worst industrial accident.

Some accidents can be prevented. Pretend that you are working for your area newspaper and choose a place in your town or school that is frequented by many people or one that has many workers. Visit that place or speak to someone who works there to determine how people keep the place safe. What is being done to prevent an accident from happening? What else could be done?

Use the space below to write your news story. Start with an attention-getting headline. Check your facts; if you quote someone, make sure you have that person's permission. And remember, your goal is to keep your public informed.

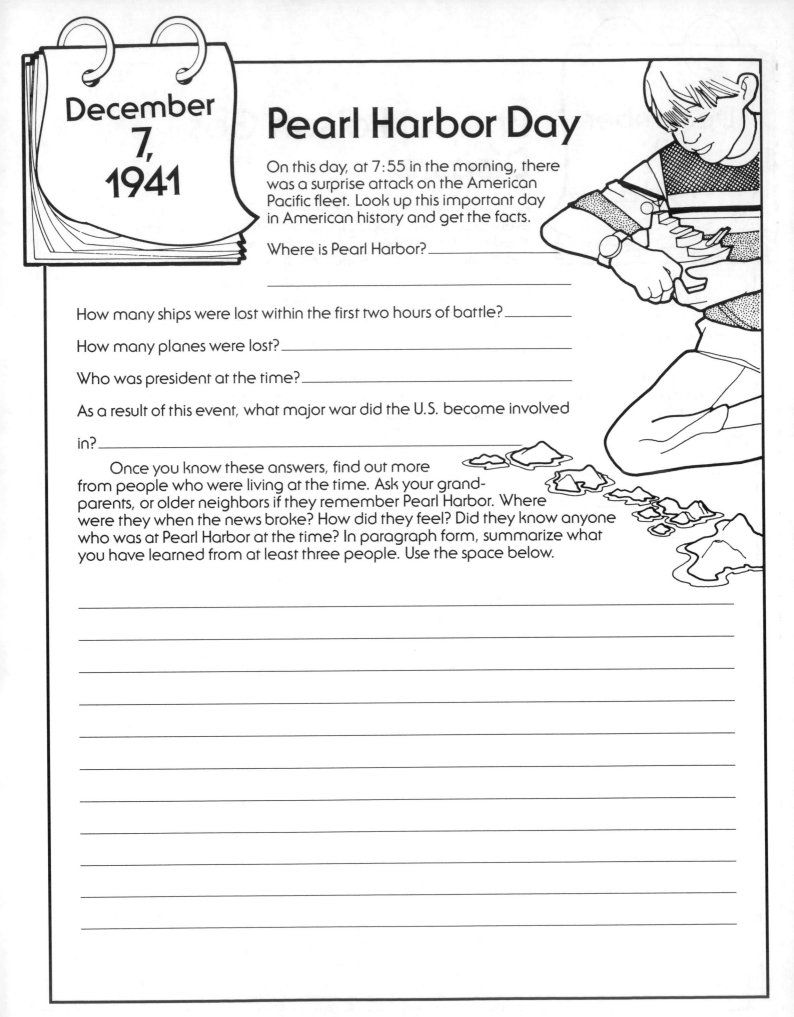

December 7, 1941

Pearl Harbor Day

On this day, at 7:55 in the morning, there was a surprise attack on the American Pacific fleet. Look up this important day in American history and get the facts.

Where is Pearl Harbor? _____

_____

How many ships were lost within the first two hours of battle? _____

How many planes were lost? _____

Who was president at the time? _____

As a result of this event, what major war did the U.S. become involved

in? _____

Once you know these answers, find out more from people who were living at the time. Ask your grandparents, or older neighbors if they remember Pearl Harbor. Where were they when the news broke? How did they feel? Did they know anyone who was at Pearl Harbor at the time? In paragraph form, summarize what you have learned from at least three people. Use the space below.

_____

_____

_____

_____

_____

_____

_____

_____

_____

_____

December 8, 1886

Diego Rivera's Birthday

If you were to travel to Mexico and visit some of its churches and community buildings, you would see at least one Diego Rivera mural. This artist painted many murals all over the country. He became famous not only for his strong colors and figures, but also for the political statements in his art. He worked very hard to express the hardships of the common people and did such a good job that some people in the government felt he should be banished from the country.

Think of an idea that people feel strongly about—pollution in the air and in the seas, endangered species, deadly diseases, or others. Below, write your ideas about it.

Issue: _____

_____

My thoughts: _____

_____

_____

_____

_____

Now try to think of a picture or a series of pictures that expresses these ideas. If you don't feel comfortable drawing the pictures yourself, cut them from magazines to make a mural collage on a large sheet of paper. Think about colors as you work. Strong, bright colors like those Rivera used have a different effect than pale pastel ones.

December 10, 1830

Emily Dickinson's Birthday

Many people who are famous today didn't become well known until after their death. This certainly was true of the poet Emily Dickinson. During her lifetime, only seven of her poems were published. After her death, 2,000 more poems were discovered by her sister Lavinia. These poems were written on the backs of envelopes and other scraps of paper locked in her dresser.

Pretend that you have just discovered an ancestor's hidden work. Is it a series of paintings? A great novel? A moving book of poetry? A piece of music?

Write a radio news announcement of this important finding. Include who, what, where, when, and why: Who was this person? Where did you find his or her work? What exactly is it? Why is it important? Why do you suggest it be shared with others?

When you finish writing, practice reading it, then present it as a radio broadcast to the class.

December 10, 1909

Anniversary of the Death of Red Cloud

This Sioux Indian has been called the only Native American who ever won a war against the United States government. Red Cloud was the son of Lone Man and Walks-as-She-Thinks. This courageous leader of the Oglala tribe fought to keep whites out of Sioux territory during the 1860s. Settlers traveling the Bozeman Trail were interfering with the main hunting grounds of the tribe. (Sioux territory was located where Montana, South Dakota, and Wyoming are today.)

In 1868, the United States government abandoned its three forts and the trail. Red Cloud lived at peace with the whites until he died in 1909. In 1987, the U.S. Postal Service issued a postage stamp honoring him in its Great American series.

Choose another person in history whom you consider a great American. Use the space below to write a paragraph about this person and your reasons for choosing him or her. Then use the back of this sheet to design a Great American postage stamp honoring that person.

Roald Amundsen Discovers the South Pole

Where's the coldest and most desolate place on Earth? Antarctica, the fifth-largest continent and the home of the South Pole. But twelve nations have research stations there, and cruise ships take tourists to see this intriguing area of the world. Everyone is discovering that Antarctica is not a frozen wasteland but a region with many resources. Offshore, the sea is rich in krill, which is a shrimplike animal that is the basis of the ocean's food chain. Some scientists believe that krill can be harvested, perhaps even as a food source for humans. The many fur seals, as well as the blue whales (the largest animals that ever lived!) are seen as valuable bounty by some people. Scientists also believe that there are large amounts of oil and valuable minerals under all that ice.

What should happen to Antarctica? Should its oil and minerals be mined? Should krill be harvested to help solve world food shortages? Should tourist travel be encouraged? Should it be left alone? What do you think? Take a stand. In the space below, write your opinion. Give at least three reasons why you think that way.

My opinion: _____

_____

_____

_____

_____

_____

Why I think the way I do: _____

_____

_____

_____

_____

December 16, 1770

Ludwig van Beethoven's Birthday

You may have heard of this famous composer who wrote music that people all over the world love. Did you know that by the age of 12 he was already a great pianist and beginning to create musical works on his own?

While Beethoven was still a young man, he moved to Vienna, Austria, where many brilliant composers were living. Soon after he moved he began to lose his hearing. By the time he was middle-aged he was totally deaf! Yet Beethoven continued to write wonderful music that the world still admires and enjoys.

What if that happened to you? What sounds would you miss hearing the most? Explain it in a paragraph.

_____

_____

_____

_____

_____

Now think of your very favorite sound—the roar of a crowd at a baseball game; rain on the roof while you're snug in bed; the chords of an electric guitar in the final measure of a song. Suppose you have a close friend who has never heard this sound before. Describe, in words, what it sounds like to you and how it makes you feel.

_____

_____

_____

_____

December 16, 1901

Margaret Mead's Birthday

Margaret Mead was an American anthropologist, a person who is an expert in the science that deals with the customs, beliefs, and development of a group of people. These customs, beliefs, and ways of doing things are called a culture. Mead studied the differences among various cultures of the Pacific Islands and the United States.

Every group has a culture. Several groups may have similar cultures. Your classroom has its own culture. Other classes in your school have similar, but not identical, cultures. Choose another class and find out some of its customs and ways of doing things. On the chart below tell how it and your own class do the following things.

	My Class	Other Class

Begin school each day: _____

_____

_____

Recognize a birthday: _____

_____

_____

Study spelling: _____

_____

_____

Ask permission to do something: _____

_____

_____

Feel about winter: _____

_____

_____

Dismiss class each day: _____

_____

_____

December 17, 1903

First Airplane Flight

After experimenting for three years with kites and gliders, two brothers, Orville and Wilbur Wright, finally succeeded in flying an engine-driven, heavier than air machine. Its small gasoline engine turned two propellers and lifted the machine a distance of 120 feet in 12 seconds. Amazing things have happened in aviation since that historic flight. Today planes can carry nearly 500 passengers and can fly at speeds faster than sound.

Get a book about airplanes from the library or look up this topic in an encyclopedia. Then put to work your ability to describe something. Select one model of airplane, historic or modern, and write a paragraph that describes it. Include all the facts you can—its size, when and where it was built, what it was used for, flying speed, advantages and disadvantages, and so on. Illustrate your paragraph. Mount your work on the bulletin board with others from the class to create a display of "Milestones in Aviation."

_____

_____

_____

_____

_____

_____

_____

_____

_____

_____

_____

_____

_____

_____

December 20, 1812

Sacagawea's Death

In 1805, a young Shoshone Indian woman, with her two-month-old baby strapped to her back, served as an interpreter and guide for the explorers Lewis and Clark as they traveled across the American continent to the west coast. It is said that the expedition would not have succeeded without her.

Sacagawea was born in what is now Idaho. As a young girl she was captured by enemy tribes and sold to a trader who made her his wife. They went to live in what is now North Dakota. Sacagawea was such a good guide because she remembered the places where her old tribe had camped and hunted and recognized them along the way.

How well do you know your neighborhood? Will you still remember it five years from now even if you move away? Close your eyes and visualize the building where you live. Then write a description of it and of the buildings on either side of it. Are they big or small? What color are they? What are they made of? What do the roofs look like? Make your description so real that people reading it would be able to recognize your house if they saw it.

December 21

Winter Solstice

Today is the official beginning of winter. What does this mean to you? What are the sounds, the smells, the sights that come to mind when you think of this special season?

Look in magazines or newspapers for words and phrases that seem to say winter to you. Cut them out. You may also find a picture or two that reflects your ideas of winter. Then arrange and rearrange your material on a large sheet of paper until it expresses your feelings about winter. Do not worry about complete sentences or lines that rhyme. Use "Winter" as the poem's title or in its ending line. Once you are happy with your arrangement, paste the material in place. Sometimes people call this patchwork poetry. Try some today.

The Third Week in December

You're Doing a Good Job Week

What a great excuse to let someone know he or she is doing a great job! Maybe it's your school custodian, your mom or dad, or the man or woman who delivers your mail. In the space below, write a note to this person. Then recopy it and deliver it to him in person. If someone comes to mind who is far away, or whom you don't want to tell in person, write her a letter of thanks or congratulations and mail it.

Dear _____,

_____

_____

_____

_____

_____

_____

_____

_____

_____

_____

_____

_____

_____

_____

The Day Before Winter Break
(December)

Remembering the Year Gone By

As this year comes to a close, think about what the year has meant to you and record your special thoughts and memories. Remember, this page can be for your eyes only. Stash this page away and get it out to read in years to come.

Year: _____

Happiest moment: _____

_____

Biggest thrill: _____

_____

Favorite book: _____

Favorite song: _____

Most admired person: _____

Saddest moment: _____

_____

One thing I learned: _____

_____

Wish for next year: _____

_____

You might want to put it in a box along with lists of favorite toys and books, a drawing of family and friends, and names of favorite athletes and musicians. Tape the box shut and put it away. Next year at this time bring it out and check to see how your ideas and interests have changed.

January 1

New Year's Day

Everybody knows what a New Year's resolution is—a promise to improve or change a habit—or try to make something happen during the upcoming year. Here's your chance to make some resolutions for other people. Pretend you have the power—what do you think reasonable resolutions would be for the following people?

The president: _____

_____

Your favorite team: _____

_____

Kids your age all over the world: _____

_____

Scientific researchers: _____

_____

Congress: _____

_____

Powerful corporations: _____

_____

You: _____

_____

_____

_____

_____

_____

_____

_____

Clio Awards

Every January, radio and television officials gather to select and recognize commercials from all over the world. What are your favorites? Why?

Commercials are a form of advertising. Advertising involves a specialized form of writing called persuasive writing. Persuasive writing tries to convince people that they need something, or should do something or should believe what the writer is saying.

Choose a product or invent one and write a commercial for it. Decide what is special about the product you've chosen and who is most likely to buy it. How can you be clever, keep the audience's attention, appeal to their interests, and still tell the truth?

Use the space below to write a script for your commercial. Will it be for radio or television? Remember, if your audience can't see the product, you'll need to approach your advertising in a more detailed way.

You might like to practice your commercial and then present it to the rest of the class. Then invite a group of judges to hear and select the five best from your room. Judges will need some guidelines to go by. Use the space below to list them, such as:

Gets audience attention quickly

Keeps audience interest throughout

January

National Hobby Month

It's National Hobby Month, so share your hobby. Use the space below to list and describe one or more of your hobbies. Tell why you enjoy these hobbies and how you became interested in them. Would you recommend your hobby to someone else? Why?

_____

_____

Take a few minutes with five people whose interests or personalities seem a lot like yours. What are their hobbies? Are there any that might be fun for you to try?

_____

_____

_____

Think about the things that interested you when you were two years younger than you are now. Then, think about the things that interest you now. Chances are you've done some changing. The world has done some changing too—and more changes are to come! In ten or twenty years you'll be more than ready for different hobbies, and society will probably offer you many more to choose from. After all, twenty years ago few people would have listed computers as a hobby.

The following questions to help you predict what you think you will be doing in the future. What hobbies and interests do you think you'll still have in five years?

Ten years?_____

_____

Twenty years?_____

_____

For the rest of your life?_____

_____

What hobbies do you hope to develop over the years?_____

_____

Use your imagination! Think about how the future will change your daily life. Now try to project future hobbies you might take up. Last of all, what hobbies would you recommend for younger children to enrich their free time?

_____

January 2, 1920

Isaac Asimov's Birthday

Isaac Asimov has written nearly two hundred books for children and adults. Many of these are science fiction. Sci-fi stories are about outer space, people from other planets, new discoveries or inventions, and what the world may be like hundreds or thousands of years from now. But science fiction is more than imagination—it describes events that could take place, based on scientific facts. Try your hand at your own science fiction story.

1. When do you want your story to take

place?_____

_____

_____

2. Where do you want it to take place?_____

_____

_____

3. Who will be your hero or heroes?_____

_____

_____

4. What will be the conflict in the story? (Suggestions: fighting for survival; overcoming lack of resources due to pollution; conquering an outer-space creature.)

Think of a beginning, middle, and end before you start writing. That way you can introduce your characters while keeping the conflict in mind. Work up to and into the conflict so you keep your readers on their toes. Keep in mind that Isaac Asimov started his science fiction writing career at age 11—you can too!

_____

_____

_____

_____

_____

January 3, 1959

Alaska State Day

What state is often called the Last Frontier? Alaska! And on this date in 1959, this last frontier became the 49th state.

What does "the last frontier" mean? What is your last frontier? Is it a place you've always wanted to explore? A place only you can discover? Close your eyes: what does your last frontier look like? Does it feel very far away? Mysterious? A little bit scary?

Your last frontier may be the farthest star in the galaxy, a hidden valley where chocolate kisses grow on trees, or some other place just inside the nooks and crannies of your imagination. Take a trip there. Use the space below to write about your journey, what this place is like, and the challenges you face as its first inhabitant.

January 7, 1854

Sherlock Holmes's Birthday

Sherlock Holmes was born on this date. Or was he? This is the birthday given to the most famous detective in fiction. He lives at 221 Baker Street in London. His landlady is Mrs. Hudson.

Create your special character. What does he or she do? Fight crime? Discover new worlds in outer space? Magically disappear and reappear elsewhere? Fill out the character description sheet below. Don't hesitate to add interesting details of your own.

Name: _____
first   middle   last

Home or place last seen: _____

Age: _____ eye color: _____ hair color: _____ height: _____ weight: _____

Birthmarks: _____

Other special characteristics: _____

_____

Favorite disguises: _____

_____

Special item of clothing or jewelry: _____

Particular fears: _____

Favorite kinds of music and books: _____

Most admired person: _____

Pets: _____

Favorite Sayings: _____

_____

Hobbies: _____

Does he or she have a personal sidekick? _____

If yes, describe: _____

January 8

Elvis Presley's Birthday

The album "Heartbreak Hotel" sold more than one million copies in just one week, and Elvis Presley was an instant star. In fact, this man, born in Tupelo, Mississippi, became the most popular American singer in the history of rock music. Between 1954 and 1959 he sold 21 million records!

Presley began his career as a country and western singer, but soon changed his style to what became rock music. He had a great influence on many other rock performers.

This kind of music was first called "rockabilly," then "rock 'n' roll." Today we know it simply as rock music. It has a strong beat and is usually accompanied by an electric guitar plus electronic equipment and speakers that produce very loud music.

Do you have a favorite rock song? Write its title below. Include a few of its lines and tell what they mean. Last of all, explain whether this is a favorite song because of the words, the melody, or the rhythm.

My favorite rock song is _____

Some of its lines are _____

_____

_____

They mean _____

_____

_____

I like it because _____

_____

_____

January 8, 1935

National Joygerm Day

Have you ever heard the expression "tongue-in-cheek"? It refers to something funny or ironic, not to be taken seriously. Some people from Syracuse, New York, started this particular day a bit tongue-in-cheek. They define "Joygerm Fever" as a wonderful, incurable disease because Joygerms chase away the blues, spread good news, and cure anyone who is down in the dumps.

Join in the Joygerm Fever! Use the space below to list 10 things you can do to chase away the blues, spread good news, or cure that down-in-the-dumps feeling for yourself and others. After you've finished writing, try out some of your ideas!

Idea	Person
1.	
2.	
3.	
4.	
5.	
6.	
7.	
8.	
9.	
10.	

January 13, 1834

Horatio Alger's Birthday

This author and clergyman wrote more than 100 books for young people and sold more than 20 million copies. He believed that the secret to success is honesty, frugality, and hard work. All the heroes of his books had these traits.

Think about the people whom you consider successful. What do you believe are their secrets of success? Write them below. Then come up with a personal motto for success.

Secrets for Success: _____

_____

_____

_____

_____

_____

My Personal Motto for Success: _____

_____

_____

_____

January 15, 1929

Martin Luther King, Jr.'s Birthday

When Rosa Parks would not give up her seat in the front of a city bus in Montgomery, Alabama, she was arrested. African-American leaders then urged people to boycott the buses (refuse to ride them). They formed an organization to support the boycott and asked Martin Luther King, Jr., to be its president. Because of his work, the city was ordered to have equal integrated seating on its buses.

Martin Luther King, Jr., also worked to fight discrimination against black people in other places—schools, hotels, restaurants, even in the voting booth. In 1963, he led a huge rally in Washington, D.C., to call attention to unemployment among African-Americans. A famous speech he gave there was called "I Have a Dream." In this speech he said, "I have a dream that one day this nation will rise up and live out the true meaning of its creed: 'We hold these truths to be self-evident; that all men are created equal.'" Finally, in 1964, Congress passed the Civil Rights Act, which prohibited racial discrimination in public places and called for equal opportunity in employment and education.

Think about King—who he was, what he fought for, and what he accomplished. Then write, in your own words, what you think Martin Luther King, Jr.'s dream was and whether or not it has come true.

January 15, 1929

Martin Luther King, Jr.'s Birthday

Martin Luther King Day is a holiday for all U.S. government employees. It is one of ten federal legal public holidays designated by the President and Congress. These are New Year's Day, Martin Luther King Day, Washington's Birthday, Memorial Day, Independence Day, Labor Day, Columbus Day, Veterans Day, Thanksgiving, and Christmas. There are no national holidays in the United States; each state must decide what holidays it will have. Most states, however, observe the federal holidays as well as one or more days that are special to their state. Thirty states observe Lincoln's birthday on February 12; several southern states remember Robert E. Lee on January 19; Missouri remembers Harry S. Truman on May 8; Texas Independence Day is observed in Texas on March 2.

Find out what holidays your state observes. List them here.

_____

_____

_____

_____

_____

_____

Is there a holiday that only your state celebrates? What is it?_____

_____

_____

If your state were to add another holiday, what do you suggest it be? Name your holiday and give at least two reasons why it would be a good day to observe in your state.

_____

_____

_____

_____

_____

_____

Discovery of a Mastodon

What amazing news! On January 16, 1962, two 15-year-old boys found two huge teeth buried underground in Hackensack, New Jersey. Later, scientists uncovered the rest of a five-ton mastodon that died at least 7,000 years ago.

How did this creature die? Who or what could have killed it? Write a newspaper article about the death. First look up information about these amazing creatures. Use as many facts as you can find to write your article; or combine this new knowledge with your imagination and write a fictional account (but let your readers know that this is your opinion). Either way you choose, your story is bound to be remarkable.

January 17, 1706

Benjamin Franklin's Birthday

Benjamin Franklin accomplished so many things in his life that it is difficult to list them all. He was a statesman, scientist, inventor, public leader, writer, and printer. His *Poor Richard's Almanac*, published from 1733 to 1758, was one of the most popular publications in Colonial America.

An almanac is a booklet or pamphlet, published annually. Early almanacs contained facts and tables about the seasons; hours of daylight; movements of the sun, stars, and moon; weather forecasts; and advice—important information for farmers and sailors. Almanacs are still published today, but most of them no longer forecast the weather.

In his autobiography, Franklin said that when he realized it was the only booklet most people read, he felt it was important to fill all the little spaces with sayings of instruction. Today we have forgotten his tables and weather forecasts, but we still remember those sayings which filled all the little spaces between the important days. Some of these are:

A penny saved is a penny earned.

A bird in the hand is worth two in the bush.

To lengthen thy life, lessen thy meals.

Choose one of these and tell what you think Franklin wanted to remind his readers.

_____

_____

_____

_____

Now, try your own hand at writing sayings. What ones can you write to

Emphasize eating correctly? _____

_____

Promote saving money? _____

_____

Encourage someone to study? _____

_____

Help people be happy with what they have? _____

_____

January 18, 1882

A. A. Milne's Birthday

Christopher Robin, Winnie the Pooh, Eyore, and Roo—Where would we be without Alan Alexander Milne, the creator of these classic characters? The stories of his son, Christopher Robin, and the boy's stuffed toys have been enjoyed for over 60 years.

Imagine that a favorite toy of yours comes alive. Does your new friend get you into trouble or save you from disaster? Write about your adventures together.

January 20

Inauguration Day

Every four years on this day, the president and vice president take office. They take their oaths of office during a ceremony called an inauguration. Because these are the highest offices in our land, you can imagine that it is very important that these persons swear that they will abide by a very important rule.

The president promises to preserve, protect and defend the Constitution of the United States. What if it were your responsibility to head the committee assigned to write the oath of office for the president? What promises would you include? You might look in an encyclopedia or other reference book to see just what the duties of the president are and what the Constitution allows him or her to do. Think about the qualities and responsibilities that you believe are a part of being president and then write an oath that you would want our president to take.

An oath: _____

_____

_____

_____

_____

_____

_____

_____

_____

_____

_____

_____

_____

January 26

Australia Day

When the United States won its independence from England, the British had to find another place to ship convicts when their jails became overcrowded. On this day in 1788, the first shipload of men and women reached the shores of Australia. There were 570 male and 160 female prisoners, 200 soldier guards (30 of these had wives), and a few children. The settlement they started was the beginning of the city of Sydney.

Now Australia is the sixth-largest country in the world, with a population that exceeds 16 million. Most of the people are of British descent—tea is the favorite hot drink, people drive on the left side of the road, and the official language is English.

But there is much about this country "down under" that is uniquely Australian. For example, it has many kinds of animals not found anywhere else. Below are the names of some of them. Use resource books to find out more about a few of these. Then imagine that you are a news reporter or a travel writer. On the back, write a short article for a travel brochure to help your readers get to know some of these unusual animals.

Australian animals: dugong, kookaburra, wombat, platypus, Tasmanian devil, dingo, wandering albatross, kangaroo, wallaby, koala, lyre bird, cassowary.

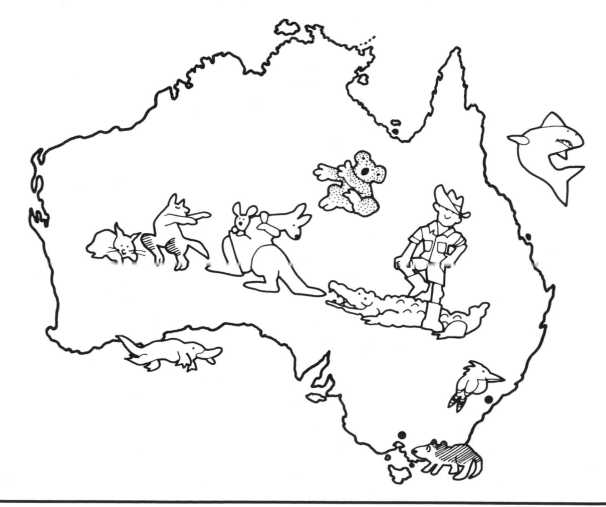

99

January 27, 1756

Mozart's Birthday

On January 27 listen to a recording of "The Magic Flute" and celebrate the birthday of Wolfgang Amadeus Mozart. This musical genius began his career as a composer at the age of five. While listening to a sample of his work, write how the music makes you feel.

_____

_____

_____

Now choose another composer—one whom you have heard about. Or ask your teacher to suggest someone. Borrow a record or tape of his or her music from the library. Write down the selection and the composer, then use this page to record your reactions to the music.

_____

_____

_____

_____

You might want to keep a record of music you have heard and how you felt about it. Start your own personal listening and feeling list. Beside each word below, write the name of the music that makes you feel sad, happy, and so on. Don't complete the list all at once. Save it and when you hear a new song, add it to your list beside the appropriate feeling.

Music that makes me feel

Sad: _____

Happy: _____

Wondrous: _____

Lonely: _____

Sleepy: _____

Energized: _____

January 27, 1973

Vietnam Cease-Fire

This was a war filled with facts and opinions. Remember that a fact is something that can be proved. An opinion is what someone thinks. See if you can get the facts about this war.

Where is Vietnam?_____

When did the war start?_____

Who was President when it began?_____

Who was President when it ended?_____

How many people were killed?_____

How many of these people were Americans?_____

What was built in Washington, D.C., to honor the people who died in the war?_____
_____

When was it built?_____

    Now for the opinions. While the war was going on, people's feelings were different from those about other wars. Do you know anyone who fought or served in the war? Ask people who remember this time to share their opinions about why feelings were so diverse and strong. Record these opinions below. What were some of the actions and events that took place as a result of these strong feelings?

Opinions:_____
_____
_____
_____

Events:

_____
_____
_____

January 31, 1919

Jackie Robinson's Birthday

Who was Jackie Robinson? Why is he considered important enough to have his birthday remembered? Jackie Robinson was the first African-American person allowed to play baseball in the major leagues. He was a skillful player, but being the first person to do something isn't always easy.

Think of a person in history who was the first person to accomplish something? If you can't think of someone, use a reference book to find such people as the first person to walk on the moon, fly alone across the Atlantic Ocean, run a four-minute mile, or become the first person of his or her sex or race to be a Supreme Court Justice. Find out as much as you can about that person and fill out the following report.

Name: _____

Where This Person Lived: _____

What This Person Did: _____

What Were Some of the Obstacles? _____

How Old Was This Person When He or She Achieved This Important Goal? _____

What Effect Did It Have on Other People? _____

_____

_____

_____

_____

_____

_____

_____

_____

_____

_____

_____

January 31, 1919

Jackie Robinson's Birthday —Continued

Another reason to remember Jackie Robinson is that he had the courage to try for something that may have seemed impossible to others. His outstanding talent and determination won him a place in the Baseball Hall of Fame.

Write about an experience in which you faced a problem for the first time. It doesn't have to be a problem that others saw as impossible, but something that was both new and difficult for you.

How did you decide what to do? Did you devise a special trick to help you overcome your fears? What was it? What advice would you offer others who may have difficulty facing or dealing with a personal problem?

Problem I Had to Face: _____

_____

_____

_____

_____

What I Did: _____

_____

_____

_____

_____

My Advice: _____

_____

_____

_____

_____

February

Children's Dental Health Month

Guess what! You've just been chosen youth chairman of Children's Dental Health Month and the President has asked you to write and design a poster to inform young children about good dental health. Use the back of this paper or a larger sheet to do just that. Before you begin, think about the information you'll need to include to make your material effective. You might want to call your dentist or ask the school nurse for any special tips and facts. Sketch out your idea in the box. Then draw the finished poster on a large sheet of paper.

You might want to share your poster with the whole class or with a younger grade in your school.

February

Black History Month

February is the month to pay particular attention to the many achievements and contributions to U.S. history made by black people. These contributions should be recalled and appreciated all year long.

Each year since 1914, a gold medal is given to the black person who has reached the highest achievement in his or her field. This is called the Spingarm Medal and recipients are chosen by a committee of the NAACP (National Association for the Advancement of Colored People). Some of the winners have been Langston Hughes, Leonytyne Price, W.E.B. DuBois, Charles R. Drew, Henry Aaron, and Alex Haley. You can find a complete list in an encyclopedia or almanac.

Choose a winner of the Spingarm Medal that you think would be interesting. Find out about his or her life and reason for winning the medal. Write at least three paragraphs about this person.

Talk to others in your class so each of you writes about a different person. Then make a copy of your story to put with all the others to make a class booklet about Spingarm Medal winners. As an introduction to the book, suggest someone (perhaps you?) write about Joel E. Spingarm and the medal that he established.

February 1, 1865

Freedom Day

On February 1, 1865, President Abraham Lincoln approved the 13th Amendment to the Constitution, which provided for the abolition of slavery. The Amendment stated that "neither slavery nor involuntary servitude, except as a punishment for crime" of which a person was convicted, would be allowed in the United States or in any territory over which the U.S. had jurisdiction.

Today is a day to think about what freedom meant to people then and what it means now. Why is freedom so important? What does the term "free citizen" mean in your life? What are you free to do under the law? What are you not free to do under the law?

After you have had some time to think about it, write a paragraph that explains what freedom means to you. Or if you wish, you might define freedom from the point of view of a prisoner in jail or a hostage in a foreign country.

_____

_____

_____

_____

_____

_____

_____

_____

_____

_____

_____

_____

_____

_____

_____

February 6, 1895

George Herman "Babe" Ruth's Birthday

As one of baseball's greatest hitters, Babe Ruth was nicknamed the "Sultan of Swat." Many other famous people are best known by their nicknames. Thomas J. Jackson is remembered as Stonewall Jackson. What would you like to be remembered for? What would your nickname be?

Nicknames are interesting. They may describe a person's appearance (Red for a red-haired person) or size or its opposite (Tiny for someone huge), a person's beliefs or accomplishments (Lightning for a swift runner), things liked (Pizza), or shorter versions of a name (Jimmy).

Select one person whom you have read about on these pages. Review what you know about him or her, perhaps look up more facts, then decide what would be a good nickname for that person. Give at least two reasons for your choice.

February 7, 1883

"Eubie" Blake's Birthday

"Eubie" Blake, a famous American musician, died February 12, 1983. He was over 100 years old! The son of former slaves, he began playing the piano when he was six. By 15, he was playing in night clubs in Baltimore. In 1921, his show "Shuffle Along" became the first black musical comedy to run on Broadway. Eubie Blake retired from show business in 1946 and spent the next 26 years writing songs. But this was a man who couldn't be pinned down. In 1969 he came out of retirement. At the age of 86, he was running on and off stage again! A new version of his show opened on Broadway in 1978 and it was so popular that the name of the show was changed to "Eubie." In 1981, President Reagan presented Blake with the Medal of Freedom, the nation's highest civilian award, at a White House ceremony.

Eubie Blake reached many important milestones in his life. Some are mentioned here. Find out more about him in a reference book. Then use the space below to construct a time line of his life, marking in these dates and any others that were significant in his life.

February 7, 1867

Laura Ingalls Wilder's Birthday

This author of the series of "Little House" books began to write them when she was sixty-five years old. Her stories tell of a pioneer family's moves to various places in the Midwest and contain excellent descriptions of everyday happenings in the life of this family. The stories are written in the third person, but are actually incidents in the life of the author as a young girl and woman. Her explanations of how the father built each cabin, how the prairie looked at sunset, how the family planted crops and cared for animals, and so on give us a good picture of just what their life was like. The television series "Little House on the Prairie" was based on ideas from these books.

Create your own "Little House" story. Think of one incident in your family's life that you enjoyed—a birthday party, a picnic, a short trip, a softball game, your first bicycle ride. Take notes about it on the lines below. Who else was with you, what did you do, what happened, where did you go? Then, on another sheet of paper, write at least three paragraphs that tell your story.

And, if you haven't read any of the "Little House" books, start one today.

_____

_____

_____

_____

_____

_____

_____

_____

_____

_____

_____

_____

_____

_____

_____

_____

The Second Week in February

National Forgiveness Week

This week has been designated as National Forgiveness Week. Take a few private moments and record actions or behaviors for which you would like to be forgiven.

Then think about forgiving someone this week, even if it's especially difficult. On the lines below tell yourself why you are angry or disappointed with this person and suggest how you will work out your feelings and show the person that he or she is forgiven.

_____

_____

_____

_____

_____

_____

_____

_____

_____

_____

_____

_____

_____

_____

_____

February 10, 1930

E.L. Konigsberg's Birthday

E.L. Konigsberg wrote *From the Mixed-Up-Files of Mrs. Basil E. Frankweiler*. If you have read the book, you know that in it a brother and sister—Claudia and Jamie—run away from home and live in the enormous and wonderous Metropolitan Museum of Art in New York City. It becomes a terrific adventure for them —sleeping in a 16th-century bed, investigating works of art in the middle of the night, dodging the watchmen. If you were to run away to a famous place and be locked in at night, where would you choose to go? Remember, there are a few necessities you'll need to take care of wherever you are—eating, bathing, sleeping. Think about the place. If you want to take someone with you, whom would you ask? What kinds of adventures might you have there? Write them in the space below. And if you haven't read *From the Mixed-Up-Files of Mrs. Basil E. Frankweiler*, look for it in your library.

The First Singing Telegram

Here's your chance. Pretend you are an employee of the Postal Telegraph Cable Company in New York City. The year is 1933 and your job is to compose the world's first singing telegram. First decide to whom you would like it to go and the message you want to get across. You could send it to the president (who was he then?), your best friend, or a relative. You might comment on politics or tell him or her you are thinking about them.

Next choose a simple tune. How about "Row, Row, Row Your Boat," or "Twinkle, Twinkle, Little Star." Figure out how many words you need for your tune and then use the space below to write your message. Try to rhyme the lines, but remember, most telegrams charge by the word, so if you want to save money, try not to go over four or five lines!

_____

_____

_____

_____

February 11, 1847

Thomas Alva Edison's Birthday

On February 11, 1847, Thomas Alva Edison was born. Probably the world's greatest inventor, he was the creator of more than 1,200 different inventions! When he could not sell his first invention, he decided never to invent anything " . .which nobody wants." His amazing mind helped him to imagine people's needs and work very hard to see what he could do to help fill them.

Now it's your turn. What do you think people need today? Your idea may be as small and useful as the safety pin, or as grand and far-reaching as the printing press. And because you want credit for your idea, you'll want to apply for a patent. A patent is a document that gives an inventor the rights to make, use, or sell a new invention.

After you're sure that you know what your invention will be, fill out the application below.

Name: _____

Date: _____

Name of Invention: _____

Purpose: _____

_____

_____

Description/Picture: _____

_____

_____

113

February 12, 1809

Abraham Lincoln's Birthday

A great many things took place in this country while Abraham Lincoln was President (1861–1865): the Civil War, the Homestead Act of 1862, the Emancipation Proclamation, the Conscription Act (white males 20–45 years old were eligible for the draft), the first income tax bill, and completion of the transcontinental telegraph, are only a few.

Pretend you are someone living during Lincoln's term—a child, a young adult, an older adult. Choose one of the events mentioned above. How did it affect you? Your family? Your future?

In the space below, write at least three journal entries about the event, from the point of view the person you have decided to be. For instance, if you are an adult who wanted his own farm, you might write about how you were successful because of the Homestead Act. Read about the Act, then tell how you got your land, where it is located, the problems you had, and so on.

Event: _____

Journal entries: _____

_____

_____

February 14

Valentine's Day

Here is a Valentine story to finish:

Chauncey Meyers was new in town. She didn't know a single person in her class and here it was February 13. How she wished that Valentine's Day fell on a Saturday, or even a Sunday. Then she could just buy her mom a card, or maybe a chocolate heart. She might even feel kind-hearted and buy her brother one, too. But nothing doing; life just wasn't that simple. There it was on the calendar—the holiday fell on a school day and that meant that every other fifth grader in Ms. Carr's class had it together because every other fifth grader had not moved here just last week. Her mom already told her that she wouldn't be allowed to be sick and made her buy and address 32 cards to hand out. Chauncey Meyers had absolutely no idea what people did here on Valentine's Day and she wouldn't let her mom call the school and ask. All she knew was that her teacher, in fact her whole class, had been conspicuously quiet all week.

Use the space below and on the back to finish this story. You might want to share your ending with others in your class and compare how different people chose to end it.

February 14

Valentine's Day

What is love? People have been asking that question over and over for many years. Why not do some asking yourself? Use the chart below to record the findings of your "What is Love?" survey. Be sure to ask people of different ages. After you've questioned at least ten people, record your own thoughts on this complicated topic below.

Name	Age	Definition or Example
1.		
2.		
3.		
4.		
5.		
6.		
7.		
8.		
9.		
10.		
11. Me		

February 15, 1820

Susan B. Anthony's Birthday

Who was she and what did she do? All you know from this page is that she was born in the early 1800s and must have done something special. Because her name is Susan, she is probably female. Start investigating. Find out why people should remember her; what she did that was illegal; how she tried to accomplish her goal, and whether she accomplished it. Write the ten most important facts you find about her below.

On another sheet of paper, create an outline for a biography you might write about her life. Decide on two or three main headings, then indicate where your facts would fit. If you cannot remember how to write an outline, look in your language arts book.

Marian Anderson's Birthday

What was it like to be a black woman singer of classical music in the first half of this century? Personally fulfilling? Probably. Easy? Never. Widely accepted? Unfortunately not.

Marian Anderson was a talented singer. She began singing in her church choir in Philadelphia, Pennsylvania, but her parents couldn't afford to give her voice lessons. So members of church groups raised enough money to send her to music school.

After studying and singing in Europe, she returned to this country and in 1936, sang for President and Mrs. Roosevelt at the White House. In 1939, she was to perform at Washington's Constitution Hall, but the organization that owns the hall wouldn't let her sing there because she was black. The U.S. government arranged for Marion Anderson to perform at the Lincoln Memorial on Easter Sunday and 75,000 people came out to hear her sing! In 1955, Anderson was also the first black performer to sing at the Metropolitan Opera in New York City. Later she served as U.S. delegate to the United Nations.

Read the summary of Marian Anderson's life again and then decide how you would have felt if you were her very best friend in 1939. Write a conversation with her showing her your pride and your support. Encourage her to not be discouraged but to continue her singing.

_____

_____

_____

_____

_____

_____

_____

_____

_____

_____

February 17, 1897

National Parent-Teacher Association

For almost one hundred years the National Parent-Teacher Association (NPTA) has been supporting education by helping parents and teachers work together in local schools. It is one of many organizations whose purposes are to increase the public understanding of education, provide school volunteers, and support special projects.

Does your school have a PTA group or other organizations? If so, write its name here.

_____

Schools that do not have an organized group often have a parent volunteer program to provide classroom and library help. Make a survey of your school. Find out what kinds of things are being done by parents and other interested individuals. On the lines below, list the work that these people do.

_____   _____

_____   _____

_____   _____

Then talk to your school principal. Find out about how many volunteers visit your school each week.

_____

Finally, talk with your teacher and others in your class to see what special project or activity a volunteer might help with in your room.
Write your suggestions here.

_____

_____

_____

_____

_____

February 18, 1848

Louis Comfort Tiffany's Birthday

This famous artist was born in New York City. His work includes intricate stained-glass windows, beautiful lamps, and even priceless doorknobs. See if you can find examples of his work. Then design your own stained-glass object or window. Illustrate it on this page and include underneath a short description for admirers or prospective buyers as if this were a page in a museum or gallery catalogue.

February 19, 1878

Patent for the Invention of the Phonograph

The phonograph is sometimes called the world's most original invention. It was so new and different. No one before had ever made any kind of a device that could "talk."

Today millions of people listen to modern versions of this invention. They hear music, poetry, speeches, books. It is a source of pleasure to many people, as well as a way to learn for blind people who listen to "talking books."

Write a letter to the phonograph's inventor, Thomas Edison, who always said it was his favorite invention. Thank him for this invention, explain what kinds of things you listen to on it, and then tell him about some of its newest refinements, such as compact discs, and how they work.

The Third Monday in February

Presidents' Day

This holiday, assigned each year to the third Monday in February, observes the birthdays of President George Washington (February 22) and President Abraham Lincoln (February 12). Many people are using the day to remember all former U.S. presidents. Choose a president and read to find some little known facts about him. Use the space below to write a riddle about your choice, using these facts. Write at least seven clues, the hardest one first, next hardest second, and so on. Read your clues aloud to the class, one at a time, to see how many are needed before someone guesses your president.

_____

_____

_____

_____

_____

_____

_____

_____

George Washington's Birthday

As President of the United States, Washington believed that the three branches of govenment should be kept as separate as possible. Find a copy of our U.S. Constitution in an encyclopedia or social studies book and read to find out what these three branches are. Then select one branch; write a brief summary of its make-up and duties.

February 26, 1802

Victor Hugo's Birthday

Victor Hugo was a famous French author. He once said, "An invasion of armies can be resisted, but not an idea whose time has come." Reread this quotation and, on the lines below, tell what you think Hugo meant.

Now think about other famous quotations you have read or heard. You might want to go to the library and ask your librarian to help you find a book of quotations. Choose one that you like and write it on the back of this page. Don't forget to include the person who said it. Then share your favorite quotation with others in your class. As a class or individually, begin to collect a book of favorite quotations and add to it all year long.

March

National Women's History Month

The National Women's Hall of Fame is located in Seneca Falls, New York. It honors women who have contributed to the development of our country through outstanding achievements in the arts, sports, education, government, science, and through humanitarian acts. Seneca Falls is the town where the first Women's Suffrage Movement convention was held in 1848.

Members of the Hall of Fame include

Abigail Adams
Jane Addams
Marian Anderson
Susan B. Anthony
Clara Barton
Elizabeth Bayley-Seton
Mary McCleod Bethune
Elizabeth Blackwell
Pearl Buck
Rachel Carson
Mary Cassatt
Carrie Chapman Catt

Emily Dickinson
Dorothea Dix Alice Hamilton
Helen Hayes
Mary Harris "Mother" Jones
Helen Keller
Belva Lockwood
Juliette Gordon Low
Barbara McClintock
Margaret Mead
Lucretia Mott
Alice Paul

Frances Perkins
Eleanor Roosevelt
Florence Sabin
Margaret Sanger
Bessie Smith
Elizabeth Cady Stanton
Lucy Stone
Harriet Beecher Stowe
Helen Brook Taussig
Sojourner Truth
Harriet Tubman
"Babe" Didrikson Zaharias.

Choose one of these women, especially one whom you have not heard of before, and write a short report on her to share with your class.

_____

_____

_____

_____

_____

_____

_____

_____

_____

_____

March

National Women's Hall of Fame

These are some of the questions that are asked about a nominee for the National Women's Hall of Fame:

What obstacles did the nominee overcome to succeed?

Will her work be remembered 25 years from now?

Was she the first woman to succeed in her field?

Are her achievements important to our country?

Who do you think should be nominated to be in the National Women's Hall of Fame? Choose your nominee and fill out the application below. Your class might like to collect these applications and vote for members in your own Women's Hall of Fame.

Name of nominee: _____

Area of outstanding achievement: _____

Description of achievement: _____

_____

_____

How does this accomplishment affect other people and our country? _____

_____

_____

How do you think she will be remembered in 25 years? _____

_____

_____

Has your nominee affected your life? If so, how? _____

_____

_____

March

National Nutrition Month

A famous nutritionist, Adelle Davis, once said, "You are what you eat." If she was right, what are you? Choose a week during this special month dedicated to selecting foods for good health, and keep track of your diet. Use the chart below and another sheet of paper to fill in meals and snacks. After you've completed your week, circle in blue everything you ate that is a member of one of the four food groups—meats, fish, poultry; dairy products; fruits and vegetables; breads and cereals. Circle in red all the junk food. Now, keeping in mind what is a good diet, use the back of this page to write a summary of your diet and list three ways that you can improve it.

Am I What I Eat?

	Breakfast	Lunch	Dinner	Snacks
Sunday				
Monday				
Tuesday				
Wednesday				
Thursday				
Friday				
Saturday				

March

March Birthdays

Albert Einstein, Casey Jones, Jane Goodall, Houdini—these are only a few of the amazing people who have March birthdays. Check an almanac and then make a list of at least twelve other well-known people who were born in March. Look over your list and next to each name, write two accomplishments that are important in today's world. Star the ones that you feel are most important.

March Birthdays	Special Qualities
1. _____	_____
2. _____	_____
3. _____	_____
4. _____	_____
5. _____	_____
6. _____	_____
7. _____	_____
8. _____	_____
9. _____	_____
10. _____	_____
11. _____	_____
12. _____	_____

March 1, 1872

The First National Park

On this day in 1872, the U.S. government created the first national park at Yellowstone. Today we have about 300 parklands. Some of these are actual parks, some are battlegrounds, homes of important Americans, monuments, recreation places, and historic sites. Many you probably have heard of, such as Glacier National Park, Crater Lake, Great Smokey Mountains, Grand Canyon. The Statue of Liberty falls under this category as a monument.

Use the encyclopedia to find out about other national parklands—choose the one you'd most like to visit, or one you have visited and enjoyed. Now design a travel brochure to encourage others to take a trip there. Don't forget to include facts about the place you're spotlighting—exact location; interesting and descriptive phrases; and perhaps, a few words of warning about protecting our environment during a visit. (Hint: Illustrations might help spruce up a brochure!)

March 3, 1931

National Anthem Day

On this day, a bill was adopted by the Senate that made the "Star-Spangled Banner" the national anthem. President Hoover signed the bill the same day. Many people love our national anthem, but others think that the words are too difficult to remember. Other people would rather have an anthem that is not centered on war or battles. What do you think? Are there any other songs that you would prefer as the national anthem? Or should a new one be written?

Try writing one yourself. You needn't worry about the music, just think about what you think America stands for—the goals and values of this country. Think about what you would like the future to be like in America and jot down some of those thoughts. Use your ideas to compile the lyrics to your national anthem and write them below. You might want to share them with your class or music teacher, or put them to music and teach the song to your class.

March 3, 1847

Birthday of Alexander Graham Bell

Born in Scotland, Alexander Graham Bell became an American scientist and educator. His father was a teacher of the deaf, and Bell worked with him in developing better ways to help teach deaf people. His experiments led to an interest in the idea of sending speech over distances.

In 1872 Bell opened a school in Boston for teachers of the deaf. He still carried on his experiments in his spare time. Thomas A. Watson helped Bell make the electrical parts for his experiments. They worked together and were friends. On March 10, 1876, the two were working in different rooms. Mr. Bell spilled acid on his trousers and called to Watson for help. Watson heard the message over the transmitter they were working with. We take the telephone for granted now, but in 1876, it was a revolutionary idea.

Do you know the correct and courteous way to make a telephone call? What are the rules you should follow? On the lines below, complete your list of rules for making a courteous telephone call. Make sure they are in correct sequence.

First, find the correct number.

_____

_____

_____

_____

Last of all, hang up the receiver gently.

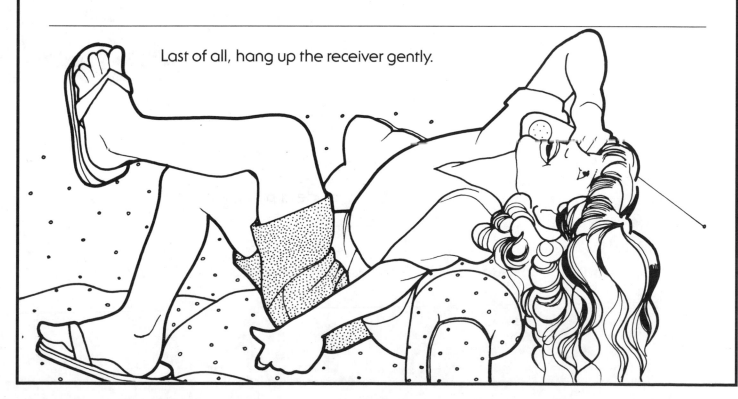

March 4, 1841

President Harrison Inaugurated

This day was a very cold and rainy one in Washington D.C. And William Henry Harrison refused to wear a hat during his inauguration—it was an outdoor cermony. Unfortunately, the ninth President of the United States caught a severe cold and never recovered from it. He died thirty days later.

In 1886, Congress passed a law that listed the order of offices that would take over in case a president and then vice-president could not serve. All of the offices are part of the President's cabinet which is another term for his special group of advisers. Below is a list of the order. Your job is to consider the current administration and find out who fills each of these positions.

President: _____

Vice-president: _____

Secretary of State: _____

Secretary of Treasury: _____

Secretary of Defense: _____

Attorney General: _____

Secretary of Interior: _____

Secretary of Agriculture: _____

Secretary of Commerce: _____

Secretary of Labor: _____ CHOO

Secretary of Health and Human Services: _____

Secretary of Housing and Urban Development: _____

Secretary of Transportation: _____

Secretary of Energy: _____

Secretary of Education: _____

Each one of the Secretaries is in charge of a specific area, has specific duties, and oversees specific services. Choose one cabinet position you would most like to have. Find out exactly what that secretary does and write a job description below.

Secretary of _____

My job involves: _____

One thing I would like to do while I am on the President's Cabinet in this position is: _____

_____

The First or Second Week in March

American Camping Week

Now that it's American Camping Week, why not plan your dream trip? Where would you like to pack off to? Idaho's Snake River to listen to the coyotes sing at sunset? Alaska, to dog-race through its wondrous frontier? The Okefenokee Swamp to watch alligators (from afar!)? What would you take with you? And who? Use the space below to write at least three journal entries about your trip—one while you are preparing to go, one describing your favorite campsite, and one that details a particularly scary, exciting, or memorable incident that happened on your trip.

_____

_____

_____

_____

_____

_____

_____

_____

_____

_____

March
20

The First Day of Spring

Though the exact time differs every year, it is on this day that the sun crosses the equator and spring begins. How would you like to bid farewell to winter and welcome the new season? You might write a poem in celebration, choose a well-known tune and come up with your own accompanying lyrics, or write a story.

Spring

Tu Bi-Shebat

Tu Bi-Shebat is celebrated in Israel each spring. It is the New Year of the Trees, or Jewish Arbor Day. Children use the day to plant trees and plants because in their culture, a tree stands for a good, strong, and noble life.

What kind of tree would you like to be? Where would you grow? Would you like to hold a treehouse? A hammock? Look over the world, as tall as a redwood? Or gently sway in the breeze as graceful as a weeping willow?

If you're not sure, look up trees in the encyclopedia to help you decide. Then use the space below to record the kind of tree you've chosen and to draw a picture of yourself. The two lines at the bottom are for you to use to write at least six adjectives which describe you. You can use the back if you'd like to write a story about your life as a tree... the things you've seen and experienced in all your years.

_____

_____

March 22, 1923

Marcel Marceau's Birthday

This man can entertain thousands of people without saying a word. Why? Because he is one of the most famous mime artists in the world. You might recognize his face—he wears very white make-up and accents his eyes with thick black pencil so that his facial expressions come across clearly. Mime artists act without words. They tell a story with gestures, movements, and facial expressions.

Marceau was born in France and loved to do pantomime as a child. He watched the movements of people and animals very closely and studied many of the silent film actors. Marceau also studied mime with a famous teacher and created his own character—Bip. Bip has made many movie and television appearances and has brought joy to people all over the world.

Try being a mime. First, decide on a particular action or incident. For instance, think about miming someone eating an ice-cream cone. First you have to take it from the serving person. Then, if you're the kind of person who would rather not get it all over your fingers, you're probably going to handle it very delicately by the end of the cone. Are you someone who likes to bite right in? Does the cold hurt your teeth? Uh-oh! It's starting to drip! Got the picture?

Now choose your activity. Think about all the steps involved: do the activity yourself or observe other people—reading the newspaper; eating a caramel apple; making an animated phone call (you'll need to imagine what the people are talking about). Use the space on this page to write down, in detail, a description of how the action is done. Look for small details in facial expressions and body positions. If possible, watch more than one person do the same thing.

After you've written down your description, take it with you in front of a mirror and practice. When you are ready, perform for a friend and see if he or she can guess what you are doing. Next, you might want to try miming a series of incidents that tell a whole story!

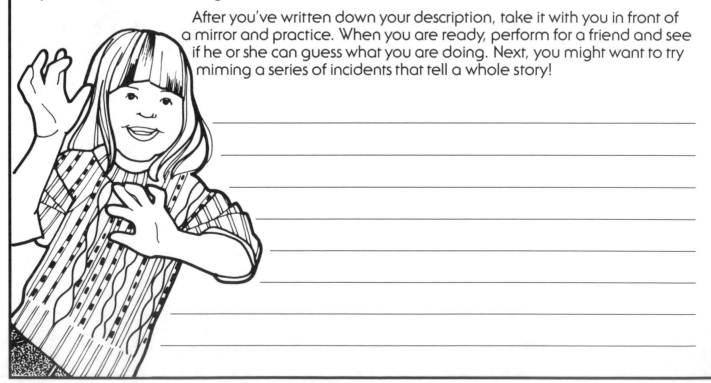

Liberty Day

On this day in 1775, Patrick Henry said, "I know not what course others may take, but as for me, give me liberty or give me death." What did he mean? Write a short play about a situation that might take place today involving a person who has those same powerful feelings. Then ask one or more friends to present your play to the rest of the class.

March 24

Museum Day

On March 24, 1937, Congress approved establishing a National Gallery of Art in Washington, D.C. It said that the gallery should belong to every citizen in the country, be open every day of the year (except Christmas and New Year's), and never charge admission.

Suppose you were to establish your own museum. What kind would it be? Would it be free? Or would the proceeds go to benefit whatever you have chosen to exhibit. For instance, if you were to have a museum about sharks, could entrance fees be used to help save the sharks? Use the space below to write a news release about your museum so the papers can let everyone in on this great opening!

Come Join Me!

My museum will be called _____

Exhibits will relate to _____

Our five most important exhibits include _____

_____

_____

_____

_____

_____

Admission information: _____

Extra details: _____

_____

_____

_____

Robert Frost's Birthday

This famous poet grew up in Massachusetts, graduated at the top of his high school class, and then dropped out of college after just a few months. He then went from job to job, trying to find something right for him. He worked in a textile mill, wrote for a newspaper, taught, and even farmed. And all the time he was trying these different occupations, he kept writing poetry. In 1912, Robert Frost left America and went to England where his first two books of poems were published. When he returned to the United States, he resumed teaching, and continued with his poetry writing.

Frost is known for using simple words and images to express ideas that he thought were important. You may have heard or read some of his poems; "Stopping By Woods on a Snowy Evening," "The Road Not Taken," "The Pasture."

In 1961, President Kennedy asked Frost to recite his poem, "The Gift Outright" at Kennedy's inauguration. This was the first time a poet had been honored in this way.

Use a separate sheet of paper, or this one, to copy one of Frost's poems. If you like, write a poem in much the same style as Frost's. Remember, your poem does not have to rhyme, but should have simple words and images, and descriptions of the scenery or countryside nearest your area. Try to subtly get across a message that is important to you, such as the importance of friendship or trust.

March 30, 1853

Vincent van Gogh's Birthday

Born in Holland, this famous artist drew and painted at least 1700 works of art. He often used bright colors and strong brush strokes in his paintings. And many people like them for this reason.

Colors have a strong influence on feelings and moods. Some people believe that bright colors make a person feel cheerful. But colors that are too bright can make some people feel confused and out of sorts. Many people find pale blues peaceful, pale pinks calming and warm. Below is a list of colors. Read the list and think of things that relate to each of the colors. Beside each color, write one or two objects in that color, and how that color makes you feel.

Bright Yellow: _____

Pale Pink: _____

Lime Green: _____

Sky Blue: _____

Fire-Engine Red: _____

Black: _____

White: _____

Pale Beige: _____

Are there any colors that particularly affect your moods—make you feel happy, calm, excited? Think about them, then decide what color you would like your classroom to be.

_____

Your bedroom: _____

Your personal and private study: _____

The First Week in April

The Week of the Young Child

An old saying goes: "You get wiser as you get older." There are many things that you have learned since you were very young.

Use the space below and write a letter to a child. Write it to a younger brother or sister, relative or friend, or to a pretend friend. In your letter, tell this younger person about the things that you have learned in hopes that your advice will make his or her life easier, fuller, and happier. Share your wisdom.

Date _____

Dear _____ ,

_____

_____

_____

_____

_____

_____

_____

_____

_____

_____

_____

_____

April 1

April Fool's Day

This special day began in France in the 1500s. Until then, the French people celebrated the new year with the coming of spring and gave presents to each other. Then, in 1564, King Charles IX adopted a reformed calendar that changed New Year's Day to January 1. Those people who still celebrated the old day were called April fools.

April Fool's Day in America begins National Humor Month. So this is the perfect time to make someone else laugh. Why not do it with a riddle? You might want to use some old favorites or look up a few new ones. Or, you might want to try writing your own. Here's a way to do just that:

First choose a subject—any subject. How about dogs? Make a list of words that remind you of dogs such as puppy, bones, bark. Take one of these words and drop the first letter (bark, drop the b, you have the sound "ark"). Think of all the word that start with "ark" such as Arkansas, or ark (the boat). Write a riddle question that relates to dogs and to one of the words you've thought of—but for the riddle, put the "b" back on. Here goes: What did Noah's two dogs call his famous boat? Noah's bark! Or how about: What state is the dog capital of the South? Barkansas!

Now, write your own riddles. Follow these steps:

1. Choose a subject.

2. Think of other words that relate to the subject and pick one of them.

3. Drop the first sound and make a list of words that begin with what is left.

4. Put back the part you dropped on each of the words.

5. Make up the riddle question using relevant facts and definitions of the word.

Choose your favorite riddles and make April Fool's cards to give to friends or relatives. Put the question on the outside and the answer along with your good wishes inside. Your illustrations will make the cards even better!

_____

_____

_____

_____

April 2

International Children's Book Day

This particular day was chosen to be International Children's Book Day because it is also the birthday of Hans Christian Andersen. Andersen was born in Denmark in 1805 and In his life wrote more than 150 fairy tales, including "The Ugly Duckling." To commemorate this day and Andersen's birthday, try your hand at writing a fairy tale.

In many fairy tales, the hero or heroine leaves home to seek a goal. After various problems or adventures, usually three, he or she achieves the goal or wins the prize. Often the prize is a princess or prince as a marriage partner.

In some other kinds of fairy tales, an animal (ugly duckling) or inanimate object (tin soldier) takes on human qualities and has many problems before it reaches a goal or finds happiness.

Decide what kind of fairy tale you will write, then let your imagination be your guide. Have fun!

Once upon a time...

April 3, 1783

Washington Irving's Birthday

This great American author was one of this country's first writers to be known all over the world. Two of his most famous stories were *The Legend of Sleepy Hollow* and *Rip Van Winkle*. In the latter story, Rip lays down for a little nap and wakes up 20 years later! Boy, have things changed!

And now it's your turn to be Rip. Imagine that it's a cozy Saturday afternoon and you decide to catch a few winks on the couch before dinner. And before dinner is just when you awake, only like Rip, it's 20 years from now. How would you know? What kinds of problems and adventures might await you? Tell your story in the first person—from your point of view. Try to make the reader feel that he or she is there and is going through all the confusion and surprise with you.

April 7

World Health Day

This day commemorates the establishment (in 1948) of the World Health Organization, which is part of the United Nations. Its purpose is to help people all over the world be healthier. It helps countries develop public health services and organizes campaigns against infectious diseases. How can you be a healthier person, both mentally and physically? List at least five ways.

1. _____

2. _____

3. _____

4. _____

5. _____

Choose the two that are most important to you. How can you change these statements into action? What could you do to really improve your health? For instance, if you have written that you could be healthier if you drank less soda pop, think of a way that you could really make that happen: every time I want a soda, I'll drink fruit juice or water instead (well, almost every time). Now write a statement below that will help put your words into action.

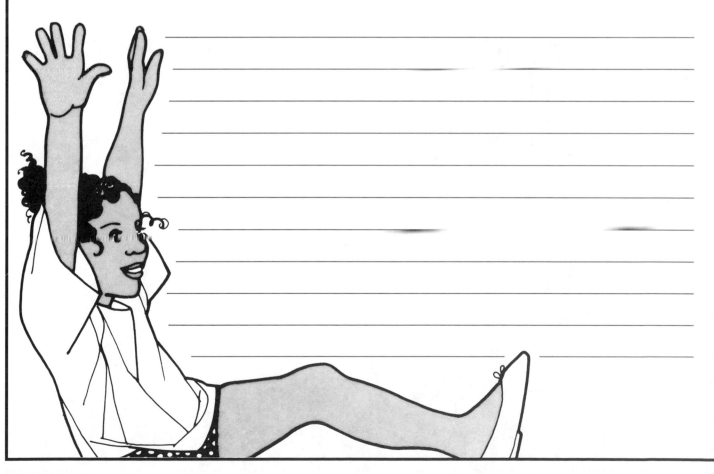

Ponce de Léon Claims Florida for Spain

The explorer Juan Ponce de Léon discovered Florida as he searched for the Fountain of Youth. There was no fountain, of course. But, what if he had found one? Peoples' lives certainly might be a lot different now! Do you think that a fountain of youth would have been a wonderful or a horrible discovery? Decide how you feel and then defend your answer in the space below.

Remember, this kind of writing is called persuasive writing. Defend your thinking and also try to get others to agree with you. To make your writing more effective include not just reasons that support your position but specific examples of what might have happened should the fountain of youth have been a reality. Don't forget to summarize your thoughts and end with a strong, persuasive statement.

After you've finished writing, read your papers to each other. Were good points brought up by other people that you hadn't thought of? Was anyone persuasive enough to change your mind?

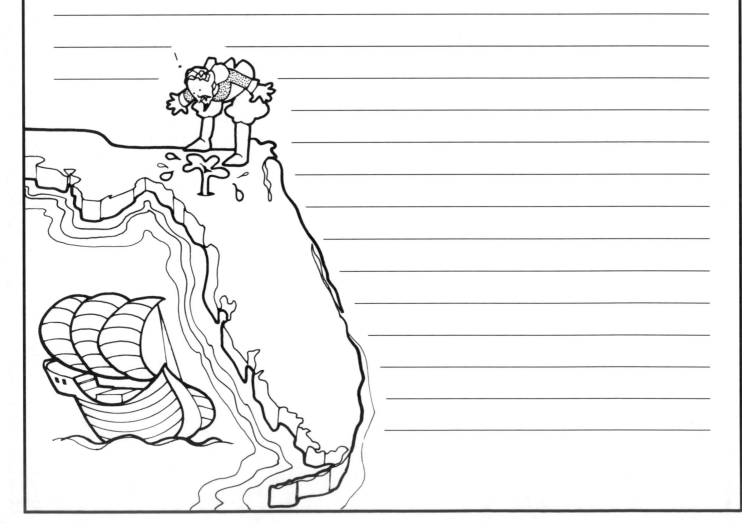

April 8, 1513

Flower Festival in Japan

Many people of Japan belong to the Buddhist religion. Today they commemorate the life of Buddha, the man who founded this religion. There are ceremonies in temples and many flower festivals. Flowers are an important part of Japanese life.

Use the front and back of this paper to list all the flowers you know. How many can you think of without using reference books? How many more can you add to your list when you refer to encyclopedias and other sources?

After you've completed your list decide which flower is your favorite. And in honor of wisdom, the quality people think was Buddha's strongest, write a Japanese haiku about your favorite flower. (Remember, a haiku is a form of poetry that has three lines with five, then seven, then five syllables in each line.)

April 14, 1912

The Sinking of the Titanic

In the early morning of April 15, 1912, the ship, *Titanic*, sank after hitting an iceberg. A lookout saw the iceberg but the ship was going too fast to avoid it. Another ship nearby ignored the *Titanic*'s distress signals. Many lives were lost.

A man named Lawrence Pringle wrote a book called *Great Mistakes*. In it, he says that mistakes are made because people 1) lack knowledge; 2) ignore the facts; 3) take a chance; and/or 4) lack planning. Obviously, when it came to the *Titanic*, many mistakes were made.

Think of five mistakes—ones that you have made or mistakes in history that you are aware of. A personal mistake might be not taking care of your dog and, as a result, the dog got lost. Most people consider the space shuttle explosion in 1986 as a great mistake in history.

List your ideas below.

1. _____

2. _____

3. _____

4. _____

5. _____

Now look over your list and look back at Pringle's reasons. Are his reasons appropriate for any of the mistakes that you have listed. Write the number or numbers of the reasons next to the mistakes. Do you think being aware of these reasons may be able to help prevent mistakes too?

April 15, 1452

Leonardo da Vinci's Birthday

This is a man who ranks as one of the most brilliant people in history. Da Vinci was an Italian painter and scientist. He studied and drew the human anatomy and objects in nature. He filled books with sketches of hundreds of inventions and designs for many machines. Take time to read more about him and his amazing accomplishments. Write a summary of the things that he did and decide if you agree or disagree with the statement of his outstanding brilliance.

April
16,
1947

Kareem Abdul-Jabbar

This man has been called one of basketball's greatest superstars. He was born with the name Ferdinand Lewis Alcindor, Jr., but changed his name when he entered the Muslim faith in 1968.

When Kareem was 13 years old he was already 6'8". By the time he entered college at the University of California at Los Angeles he was at his full height of 7'2"! Kareem Abdul-Jabbar had led many teams to championships but in 1968 he refused to play on the U.S. Olympic team as a protest of the way America treated African-Americans.

Kareem is an excellent role model for young people. Many athletes today serve as role models for the rest of society and especially for kids. The way they act and the things that they do, in or out of the sport, show they are responsible people who believe their actions should match their athletic abilities.

Pretend you are the editor of a newspaper. Write an editorial discussing the statement: A professional athlete has a responsibility to the public (and especially to young people) to be a good role model.

Before you begin to write, decide what you think a good role model is and does. Remember, this is a personal opinion piece but you can ask others how they feel and think. You might want to prove your point by including examples of other sports figures who act responsibly.

April 18, 1906

San Francisco Earthquake

On this date in 1906, forces from the Earth's interior caused layers of the Earth to squeeze together and then stretch. This resulted in a catastrophic earthquake which then caused a fire that leveled most of the city of San Francisco and killed over 700 people.

A second, very serious earthquake in San Francisco and the neighboring area occurred on October 17, 1989. Many buildings were ruined and a bridge and freeway collapsed. Many people were killed.

Many schools in the United States have earthquake drills; some schools have tornado drills; every school has fire drills. These safety procedures are very important for everyone to know.

Use the space below to write the instructions that should be followed in your room if the fire bell should go off. First, go over the steps in your mind, check with your teacher or instructions posted in your room, and then write. This way you can make sure that your directions are orderly and clear.

On the back of this paper write a set of instructions for another safety procedure that may be practiced in your school such as an earthquake drill, a tornado drill, or someone choking in the lunchroom. Aim for clarity!

The Last Week in April

Canada—U.S. Goodwill Week

Canada and the United States have been peaceful and friendly neighbors for a long time. There are many similarities as well as differences between the two countries. Use resource books to fill in these facts about the two countries.

	CANADA	USA
Political Divisions	_____	_____
Kind of Government	_____	_____
Kind of Money	_____	_____
Kind of Measurement	_____	_____

Depending on which country you live in, where in the other country would you like to visit?

_____

_____

Look up the other country and write down at least five things you learned that you didn't know.

_____

_____

_____

_____

_____

_____

_____

_____

The Third Monday in April

The Boston Marathon

The first Boston marathon was held in 1897 and it has taken place every year since then. It is the oldest race of its kind in America. The first winner was John J. McDermott, who ran the 26 miles and 385 feet in 2 hours, 55 minutes, and 10 seconds.

Find out the exact date of the marathon this year and do a news report on it. Fill in your readers, or listeners (whoever you decide your audience will be) on some of the changes that have taken place in the marathon over the years. Why is it always held on the third Monday in April? What happens if it rains? Can there be more than one winner? Are there different divisions for contestants? What was last year's fastest time? This year's? You may have to refer to news magazines or newspapers to find your answers. Use an encyclopedia to find out why a marathon race is 26 miles and 385 feet in length.

Use the back of this paper to write your news report.

April 21, 1838

John Muir's Birthday

John Muir's love of nature led him to explore lands all over the world. He persuaded President Theodore Roosevelt to protect 148 million acres of forestland in the United States. Muir also founded the Sierra Club—an organzation dedicated to protecting the environment.

Be an explorer like Muir. What are places you have read about or seen pictures of—a tropical deserted island; the tall, mysterious peaks of the Himalayas; a jungle path near the Amazon River? List five that you might like to see:

1. _____

2. _____

3. _____

4. _____

5. _____

Choose one and look up more about it in an encyclopedia or other reference books. As you read about this special place try to picture it in your mind's eye. What colors do you see? Is there a breeze? How does it feel? What kind of shelter would you need if you were to stay there for a while? What kinds of food would you live on? What would your life be like, even if you stayed only a month? Use the space below and attach other pages to write at least three journal entries. Include ways that you would try to preserve the environment during your stay.

_____

_____

_____

_____

_____

_____

_____

April 22

Arbor Day

Though Arbor Day is celebrated on different dates in different localities, it officially began in Nebraska on April 10, 1872. It was promoted so well by J. Sterling Morton, a newspaper publisher, that over a million trees were planted that day in Nebraska. When Mr. Morton died, Nebraska moved the day to April 22, his birthday. The day is still celebrated close to this date. It is a day to honor and plant trees. In his book *The Giving Tree*, Shel Silverstein writes about the ways in which trees are our very good friends.

Think about it, they certainly do make our world more beautiful, especially at this time of year. And there are many foods and other products that come from trees.

Try to imagine our world without trees. What would it look like? What would we miss? What might we have to live without? Pretend you've just gotten up—it's a school day, and it seems like any other. But something is different. All of the trees are gone!

Draw a picture of what your neighborhood or a local park would look like without trees.

April 27, 1906

A New Town Is Built

On this date United States Steel Corporation began building a huge steel plant in the Midwest—halfway between the iron-ore mines and the field of coal that would be needed to run the smelting furnaces to make the steel. But the plant needed workers and those workers needed homes nearby, so the company built a town too. And that town became Gary, Indiana.

What if you were in charge of building a town—what an incredible responsibility—and an exciting challenge! Here's your chance. Where would your town be? In the mountains? By the ocean? How would the people make their living? What facilities would you have to provide? And thinking back to Gary, what kind of environmental protection would you build into the site? How many people would you want to live in your town? Any special kinds of transportation? Parks? Museums? What would be special about your school system? Describe the government in your town?

_____

_____

_____

_____

After you and your classmates have answered these questions, design a brochure to get people to move to your town. Experiment with ways of folding a plain sheet of paper so that you will have room to say what you'd like and also so that it will capture the curiousity of your reader. Remember your objective is to convince each person that this is a place where he or she might like to live, could benefit from, and could contribute to. Keep it realistic but make it exciting!

April 30, 1904

Louisiana Purchase Exposition

What happened on this day, at this exposition? Something that affected all of our lives—the introduction of the great American staple—a hamburger patty in a bun! And since then, these meaty wonders have been fixed in all sorts of ways and sold at all sorts of restaurants.

But go back to that day in history and pretend that you are the person that the busy cook gave this new concoction to. Pretend that when you got home from the fair, your grandmother asked what you saw and did at the fair. Tell her you tried a new way to eat hamburg steak. Describe how it looked and tasted. (It probably did not have ketchup or relish on it. Those things came later.) Then explain how it was made and decide whether or not you'd like to try it again. Another food that became popular at this fair was the ice-cream cone. Maybe you'd like to describe it too. Remember, your grandmother has never seen one.

_____

_____

_____

_____

_____

_____

_____

_____

_____

_____

_____

_____

May

Mental Health Month

May is Mental Health Month. You know that doctors often write prescriptions to help people feel better physically. But good mental health can be just as important. Good mental health is feeling fine about yourself, your life, and your relationships with other people.

Use the prescription form below to write your personal advice on how to feel healthy mentally. Include healthy tips, suggestions you have read about, and any other good advice that relatives or friends have given you.

From Dr. _____

Goal: Good Mental Health

Prescribed Methods and Advice: _____

_____

_____

_____

_____

_____

_____

_____

_____

_____

_____

May

National Sight-Saving Month

National Sight-saving Month is sponsored by the National Society to Prevent Blindness. Its goal: to encourage people to take care of their eyes, get checkups, and take safety precautions.

Unfortunately, many people are blind—some were born that way and others developed this disability sometime during their lives. What if you were blind? Having seen the many sights that you have seen, what do you think you'd miss the most?

Pretend that you have been given the opportunity to help a blind person your age "see." Choose one of your favorite sights—a rainbow or sunset; a mischievous puppy; pizza, fresh out of the oven.

Now jot down everything you can about this scene. Think of colors and textures and write the most descriptive paragraph you can—but don't mention the name of the object. Read your description to a classmate. Can he or she guess what you are talking about? What would your classmate add to the description to make it more accurate?

_____

_____

_____

_____

_____

_____

_____

_____

_____

_____

_____

The First Week in May

Be Kind to Animals Week

Have you ever read about Dr. Dolittle? He is an animal doctor created by the author Hugh Lofting. In all the books about Dr. Dolittle one important characteristic stands out: he can talk to the animals!

If you could talk to an animal, which one would you choose? And what would you like to talk about? Think about your choice of animals and the questions you would like to ask. Use the space below and the back of this paper to write a conversation between you and the animal. Don't forget, there just may be questions that animal might like to ask you!

The animal of my choice: _____

_____

_____

_____

_____

_____

_____

_____

_____

_____

_____

First Week in May

National Pet Week

Pets are wonderful, aren't they? This is the week to celebrate just that. It's not always easy to be a good owner, and it's not always easy to be a pet.

Think about your pet, or a pet you would like to have—a clumsy, furry puppy; a three-foot-long turtle whose back you could ride on; a baby elephant. Use your library and other reference books to find out as much as you can about your real or imaginary pet. What's the best environment? The best food? Important care and cleanliness facts to keep this animal in the best of health? Use the space below to write a list of rules and helpful hints about how to keep this pet healthiest and happiest.

May 1

Start of Gazpacho Aficionado Time

What's an aficionado? Someone who is an enthusiastic admirer of something. You could be a dog aficionado, a baseball aficionado, or even a popcorn aficionado.

Now, what's gazpacho? Gazpacho is a Spanish word (so is aficionado) that refers to a cold soup made from tomatoes, other vegetables, and spices. This month begins Gazpacho Time because tomatoes are just beginning to get ripe in many parts of the world.

Try making gazpacho. It's good for you, but more important, it tastes good. Here's a recipe that you can modify to suit your taste. It's easy enough to make at school, but maybe you'd rather take this recipe home and prepare it for your family. It makes enough for eight people.

    6 large ripe tomatoes
    2 red or green peppers (cored and seeded)
    2 medium-size onions
    2 cucumbers (peeled and seeded)
    1 1/2 cups tomato juice
    1/2 cup vinegar
    1/2 cup oil
    pinch of cayenne or pepper
    salt
    dill

Wash and chop the vegetables. (Be very careful with the knife.) Keep the juice that is released when you chop the tomatoes and mix the tomato juice, oil, and vinegar. Puree a small portion of the vegetables and part of the liquid together in a blender. Mix with the rest of the vegetables, the rest of the liquid, stir in a little cayenne or pepper, salt, and dill. Cover and chill for a couple of hours. Enjoy!

May 1

Gazpacho Time Continued

Now start your own international cookbook. Use this gazpacho recipe to represent Spanish cooking. Find recipes for dishes from other countries and cultural heritages.

Perhaps your class can make a book together: Have each person choose a country or group. Try to find foods from such countries as China, Japan, France, England, Italy, Russia, Mexico, and Greece. Combine the recipes and make a copy of the class book for everyone.

Write one of your recipes here:

HINT: A good source of recipes is an older family relative or friend or that person's well-worn cookbook.

_____

_____

_____

_____

_____

_____

_____

_____

_____

_____

_____

_____

_____

_____

_____

May 1-8, 1704

First Advertising Space

The first advertising space ever sold in a newspaper was in one column, four inches deep in the *Boston News-Letter*. There were three ads. One ad offered a mill with a plantation, a large brick house, and another good house.

Pretend you are a real estate agent. Create two newspaper real estate ads for a house you want to sell. Before you write the ad, imagine what the house is like, where it's located, and what it looks like inside and out.

FOR SALE

PRICE $350

Location: _____

Number of rooms: _____

Special features: _____

_____

_____

_____

_____

_____

What is the surrounding area like? _____

Now write your ads. First create a display ad about 4" x 6". Use colorful, persuasive words. You might include a drawing of the house. Then write a classified ad. Classified ads charge by the word, so you will need to tell your story as briefly as possible. For instance, instead of saying, "There are three large bedrooms," just say, "Three bedrooms." See how much you can say in 12 words or fewer.

Include a drawing or photograph on this page or attach another sheet. Using this information, create a newspaper ad for your house.

_____

_____

_____

_____

_____

_____

_____

May 1

Law Day

Why do we have laws? And what place do they hold in our everyday lives? Those are a few of the questions to ask yourself on Law Day.

Do you think there should be fewer or more laws? Why? Which ones would you abolish? What would you add? Write your list below.

Share your list with other members of your class and work together to compile a class list of laws that protect and work for you every day.

_____

_____

_____

_____

_____

_____

_____

_____

_____

_____

_____

_____

_____

_____

_____

_____

May 5

Urini Nal

Republic of South Korea has a holiday known as Urini Nal that is a special holiday for children. It began in 1919 when a man named Chung Hwan Bang felt that children should have one day all their own in return for being obedient the rest of the year.

Schools close so that parents can plan special activites. A Children's Park is in Seoul, the capital of South Korea, and on this day the admission is free. There are puppet shows, dancing, wrestling and martial arts exhibitions, and tugs-of-war. Plus, there are many good things to eat, such as popcorn, barbequed meats, hot dogs, rice cakes, and one special treat made with pickled cabbage, pine nuts, and chestnuts. Many families attend free movies or theater events before the day is over.

Pretend that today is a special holiday just for you. Use the space below as you would a page in a diary. Record how you celebrated your special day. Where did you go? Whom did you meet? What special treat did you cook up for yourself? Remember, this is your day—the sky is the limit!

Date: _____

Dear Diary, _____

_____

_____

_____

_____

_____

_____

_____

_____

_____

_____

_____

_____

_____

The First Saturday in May

Kentucky Derby

On the first Saturday in May people come from all over the world to watch the most famous horse race in America—the Kentucky Derby. It's been run each year at Churchill Downs in Louisville, Kentucky, since 1875.

Many people have mixed feelings about horse racing. Some are worried that the horses are not cared for properly. Others say that because these horses are so special they are loved and treated with the utmost care. Some people feel that horse racing encourages betting. Others believe that it is a fine sport to enjoy.

Try your hand at writing both sides of the argument. Pretend that you are an owner who has groomed a very special horse for racing and the governor of your state is considering banning horse racing completely. Think of at least three good reasons racing should continue and write the governor a letter defending your position. On the other side of this page, pretend that you are the governor. Thank the owner for the letter and explain your reasons for considering banning horse racing.

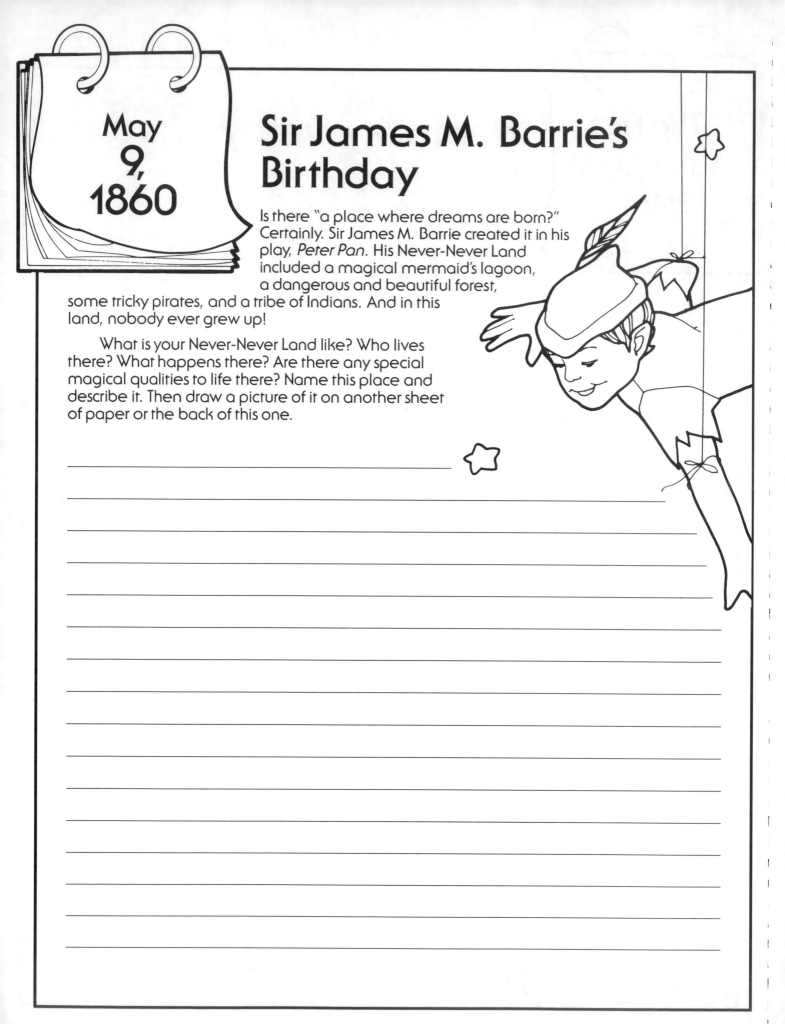

May 9, 1860

Sir James M. Barrie's Birthday

Is there "a place where dreams are born?" Certainly. Sir James M. Barrie created it in his play, *Peter Pan.* His Never-Never Land included a magical mermaid's lagoon, a dangerous and beautiful forest, some tricky pirates, and a tribe of Indians. And in this land, nobody ever grew up!

What is your Never-Never Land like? Who lives there? What happens there? Are there any special magical qualities to life there? Name this place and describe it. Then draw a picture of it on another sheet of paper or the back of this one.

May 13, 1950

Stevie Wonder's Birthday

This blind musician recorded his first hit when he was only 12 years old. And since then he has recorded hit after hit—songs and albums! When Stevie Wonder became involved in the movement to make Dr. Martin Luther King, Jr.'s birthday a national holiday, he recorded the song "Happy Birthday." And this important singer would love it if there were a party for world peace on King's birthday every year.

If you were the host or hostess of this world-peace party, who would you invite? What would you serve? What would be some topics of conversation at the tables? (Take it for granted that there will be interpreters so that people from all cultural backgrounds can understand one another's languages.) As the host or hostess, it's up to you to make the closing remarks to your guests. What thoughts would you leave them with as they head back to their homes?

_____

_____

_____

_____

_____

_____

_____

_____

_____

_____

_____

The Second Sunday in May

Mother's Day

In the countries of Denmark, Italy, Turkey, Belgium, Australia, and the United States, Mother's Day is celebrated the second Sunday in May. In Africa, it is the first Sunday. People in Argentina celebrate it in October, and Norwegians celebrate it in February.

In France, Mother's Day is a family holiday. The whole family gathers for a wonderful, large meal together, and after the meal is over, all the mothers in the family receive a cake that looks like a beautiful bunch of flowers.

In Sweden, the Red Cross makes the holiday special for certain mothers. They sell plastic flowers to raise money to send a few deserving mothers on vacation!

Obviously people through most of the world think that there should be a Mother's Day holiday. It's just when and how to celebrate it that makes the difference.

If you could do anything for your mother or a female relative or friend to celebrate Mother's Day in a special way, what would it be? Take a few minutes to think and then describe this treat below.

May 16

Biographers' Day

It was on this day in 1763 that two men, James Boswell and Samuel Johnson, met in London. Boswell kept numerous journals and notes about Johnson and his life. After Johnson's death, Boswell completed the story of his life. It is looked upon as a model of biographical writing. This day celebrates the particular form of writing that tells the story of another person's life.

If you were to write a biography who would be your subject? Many authors prefer to write a biography of someone who is still alive. That way the author can interview the person and also his or her friends and colleagues. These interviews often provide a truer and fuller picture of the person.

Write a biography of someone you know and admire. Gather your facts, interview the person, ask if you may talk to other people your subject knows (you might want to ask for specific suggestions). As you ask questions about this person's life, look for an incident that stands out as important. You might begin your biography with that incident and continue your writing by filling the reader in on what took place before and afterward.

You might want someone else who knows the person to write an introduction to the biograaphy. When completed you might give your work to the person you are writing about.

Academy Awards

The first Academy Awards were given on May 16, 1929, for achievements in films made during 1927–1928. To give them, people had to decide what makes one movie better than another. The script? The actors? The impact on the audience? Or all of these and more? Use the space below to list five criteria, or tests, you would use if you had been a member of this first Academy of Motion Picture Arts and Sciences.

Motion Picture Arts and Sciences Criteria for a Good Movie

1. _____

2. _____

3. _____

4. _____

5. _____

Now list five of your favorite movies.

1. _____

2. _____

3. _____

4. _____

5. _____

Pretend you will write, direct, and produce a movie today. What is it about? Who would you like to star in the main roles?

_____

_____

_____

_____

May 20-21, 1927

Lindbergh Transatlantic Flight

On a rainy morning in a muddy field at Roosevelt, New York, Charles Augustus Lindbergh took off. He was 25 years old and was flying a plane called the *Spirit of St. Louis* on the first solo flight across the Atlantic Ocean.

If he made it—flying nonstop between New York and Paris— he would win a prize of $25,000! Some called him the Flying Fool; others preferred Lucky Lindy. And Lucky Lindy he was. He flew the distance—3,600 miles—from New York at 7:52 a.m. on May 20 to Paris at 10:24 p.m. on May 21. Lindbergh was an instant hero!

Pretend you were either at the airport in New York, at the airport in Paris, on board the plane with him, or even Charles Lindbergh himself. Write the story of this adventure. Depending on who you've decided to be, fill in the story with as much personal feeling and facts as you can.

Here's the extra challenge—keeping in mind that Paris time is six hours ahead of New York time, figure out how long it took Lindbergh to make the flight. And if you're really feeling ambitious, remember that he flew 3,600 miles in all and find the average number of miles per hour that he flew! Good luck!

May 22, 1844

Mary Cassatt's Birthday

Mary Cassatt was one of America's most famous women painters. She moved to Paris when she was in her twenties and joined the French movement of Impressionist painting. At that time, these paintings were brighter and lighter than those of other styles, and most portrayed everyday people and daily life rather than royalty or historical events. Cassatt became famous for her paintings of mothers and children and family scenes.

Now you have a choice. You can look up an Impressionist painting, by Cassatt or another Impressionist artist, and write a description of it on the lines below. (Don't forget to include the name of the painting, the artist, and the year it was painted.)

Or, you can choose an everyday scene to observe—kids out playing ball, a child reading under a tree. Take time to look at the colors—the sky, the leaves on the trees and blades of grass, the way a sunny sky makes all the colors look brighter or the way the sky darkening before a rainstorm can make all the colors look deeper. In the space below, try to describe the scene, using the most descriptive words possible. On another sheet, become an Impressionist artist and portray your scene colorfully. Don't forget to sign your work and give it a title.

_____

_____

_____

_____

_____

_____

_____

_____

_____

_____

_____

May
24,
1819

Birthday of Queen Victoria

Queen Victoria was queen of the British Empire for 63 years. While she was queen, the colonies of British North America were united to become the Dominion of Canada. So, on the Monday before May 24 each year, Canadians celebrate Victoria Day. They remember this famous queen and also use the day to honor the present-day king or queen of the British Commonwealth of Nations.

During Victoria's reign, the British Empire reached its greatest power. In an encyclopedia or other reference book, read about some of the things that occurred during her reign—expansion of the British Empire, events in the history of Canada, literature of the period, accomplishments of her nine children and numerous grandchildren, growth of industry, and so on. Pick one topic and write notes about it on the lines below. On a separate paper, write three paragraphs that tell about your topic, using your notes as guides.

The Fourth Week in May

Cartoon Art Appreciation Week

Everyone loves a good cartoon. Some people cut out their favorites and keep them in a scrapbook to look back on and enjoy over and over again. But all cartoons aren't designed just for enjoyment; some make a political statement by using a humorous drawing to call attention to some situation. Take a look at a newspaper tonight. Read the funnies and also look on the editorial or opinion page to see if there are any political cartoons. Ask someone in your family to help explain the cartoon's meaning if you're not sure what the cartoonist meant.

Now decide what kind of cartoonist you would like to be. Do you want to make up your own cartoon around a character who already exists? Do you want to create a new character or illustrate a favorite riddle? Do you want to try drawing your own political cartoon? Use the space below and the reverse side of this page for practice. When you have got just the look, the lines, and clarity you want, copy your cartoon over on plain white paper and share it with your class. You might want to put together a class book of cartoons or carry on your own character in a series of adventures or humorous incidents.

May 28, 1888

Jim Thorpe's Birthday

Jim Thorpe was born near Prague, Oklahoma. His Indian name was Wa-Tho-Huck (Bright Path). While growing up, he and his twin brother, Charlie, challenged each other to tests of strength and speed. And they were admired for being the best in their tribe. No one in history has ever achieved as much in so many sports as Jim Thorpe. And in 1950, three years after his death, leading sports editors voted him the greatest athlete of the first half of the 20th century. In 1977, a similar vote by sports editors and columnists again placed him at the top of the list.

The story of Jim Thorpe's life is fascinating—from childhood through adulthood. Look up information in a sports book, or find a biography of him. After you have read the events that shaped his life and his accomplishments, list his most important ones.

Now try your hand at ballad writing. A ballad is a poem that tells a story and is often set to music. Some ballads have a chorus that is sung between every verse. Many ballads are written about people who have accomplished amazing feats. Use the space below or on the back of this sheet of paper to write a ballad about the life of Jim Thorpe.

May 30

Memorial Day

Memorial Day, observed the last Monday in May, honors those who have died fighting for our country. During the Civil War, Southern women often spread flowers on the graves of both Union and Confederate soldiers. In 1866, a memorial service was held in Waterloo, New York, to honor those who had given their life for their country. In 1868, the head of the Grand Army of the Republic, a Civil War veterans' group, asked its members to hold Decoration Day ceremonies and to decorate the graves of comrades. May 30 was set aside as that day. Today we use the day to remember those who have served and died in all the wars of this country.

Read your local newspaper or listen to radio and television reports for facts about the Memorial Day observance in your community. Perhaps you can attend. Then describe, in a letter to a friend or a news article, how your community honored its dead servicemen on this day.

_____

_____

_____

_____

_____

_____

_____

_____

_____

_____

_____

_____

_____

Last Week in May

National Shoe Week

Did you know that the last week in May usually celebrates shoes and healthy feet? Why not be a participant? Choose your favorite shoe—a good old comfortable sneaker, a cozy slipper, a soft and shiny leather boot. Now write a story from the shoe's point of view. What's it like to be this shoe? What does the world look like from a shoe's perspective? What does this shoe do to solve a problem or help someone? And as your favorite shoe, what do you hope and dream about?

Second Week in June

National Little League Baseball Week

This organization of baseball teams for young players was organized in 1939 in Williamsport, Pennsylvania. It's players are ages 8 to 12. Both boys and girls may play. The game is played like the adult game except that the playing area is smaller and there are only six innings instead of nine.

Do you play on a Little League or other baseball team? Do you prefer some other game? Think about a game you and your friends like to play. What equipment do you need? What are its playing rules? Think about them. Now pretend that you have a friend who has never seen or played the game you like. On the lines below, tell about the game and give the rules for playing it. Be very plain so that when you are done, your friend will be able to learn to play the game.

_____

_____

_____

_____

_____

_____

_____

_____

_____

_____

_____

_____

_____

_____

_____

_____

June 14

Flag Day

Did Betsy Ross really sew the first American flag? No one knows for sure. But the flag adopted by Congress on June 14, 1777, has had only a few changes since then.

What if we had no flag for our country and the President assigned you the task of designing one? Use the space below to write a brief description of what our country stands for. Then try to think of symbols and colors that illustrate what you've written. Use the back of this paper and draw your American flag design.

_____

_____

_____

_____

_____

_____

_____

_____

_____

_____

_____

_____

_____

_____

_____

June 19, 1910

First Father's Day

On this date, the first Father's Day was celebrated in Spokane, Washington. President Coolidge supported the idea in 1924, but it was not until 1966 that a presidential proclamation set Father's Day as the third Sunday in June.

Design and write a special card for Dad or any male friend or relative. First think about that person's interest or hobby. Does he like to fish or read or jog in the park or build model airplanes?

Plan your card to go with this interest. Make it in the shape of a fish, a book, a tree, or an airplane, for example, and use words connected with this hobby in your message. "I caught the big one (fish) when I got you for a Dad (friend, grandfather). Or, "As a Dad, you're the perfect model." Use your imagination. You'll make a winning card.

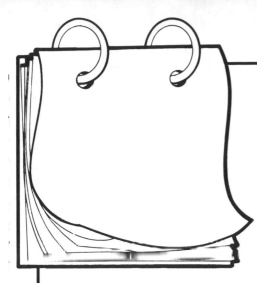

End of School

You've made New Year's resolutions. Why not make a few summertime resolutions? List at least 10 things you hope you'll do this summer— make a new friend, start a new hobby, get more exercise. And if you could do anything this summer, what would it be?

Resolutions

1. _____

2. _____

3. _____

4. _____

5. _____

6. _____

7. _____

8. _____

9. _____

10. _____

If I could do anything, I'd _____

_____

_____

_____

_____

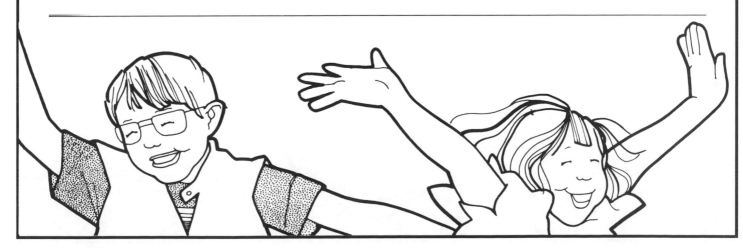

Jane Schall has taught elementary school and directed preschool programs in Ohio and Alaska. She was the features editor of *Instructor Magazine,* and is currently Editorial Director of the Early Childhood Division of Scholastic Inc. and Editor of *Pre-K Today* magazine. She loves children and misses teaching very much.

Jane is also the author of *Instructor's Big Book of Teacher Savers II.*

Patricia Briles lives in California with her husband and son and an endless parade of pets. She designs greeting cards for her family-owned business. Patricia has illustrated many books including *Instructor's Page-A-Day Pursuits; Teaching Kids to Care; Games, Giggles and Giant Steps;* and *Instructor's Big Book of Teacher Savers II.*